Eastern

and Legenas

BY.

MARIE L. SHEDLOCK

FOREWORD BY
PROF. T. W. RHYS DAVIDS

INTRODUCTION BY
ANNIE CARROLL MOORE
OF THE NEW YORK PUBLIC LIBRARY

NEW YORK
E. P. DUTTON & COMPANY
681 FIFTH AVENUE

EASTERN STORIES
AND LEGENDS

'9 WAT '09

FOREWORD

I RECOLLECT riding late one night along the high-road from Galle to Colombo. The road skirts the shore. On the left hand the long breakers of the Indian Ocean broke in ripples on the rocks in the many little bays. On the right an endless vista of tall cocoanut palms waved their top-knots over a park-like expanse of grass, and the huts of the peasantry were visible here and there beneath the trees. In the distance a crowd had gathered on the sward, either seated on the grass or leaning against the palms. I turned aside—no road was wanted—to see what brought them there that moonlight night.

The villagers had put an oval platform under the trees. On it were seated yellow robed monks with palm-leaf books on their laps. One was standing and addressing the folk, who were listening to *Bana,* that is

"The Word"—discourses, dialogues, legends, or stories from the Pali Canon. The stories were the well-known Birth-stories, that is the ancient fables and fairy-tales common to the Aryan race which had been consecrated, as it were, by the hero in each, whether man or animal, being identified with the Buddha in a former birth. To these wonderful stories the simple peasantry, men, women and children, clad in their best and brightest, listen the livelong night with unaffected delight, chatting pleasantly now and again with their neighbors; rising quietly and leaving for a time, and returning at their will, and indulging all the while in the mild narcotic of the betel-leaf, their stores of which afford a constant occasion for acts of polite good-fellowship. Neither preachers nor hearers may have that deep sense of evil in the world and in themselves, nor that high resolve to battle with and overcome it, which animated some of the first disciples. They all think they are earning "merit" by their easy service. But there is at least, at these full-moon festivals, a genuine feeling of human kindness, in harmony alike with the teachings of Gotama and with the gentle beauty of those moonlit scenes.[1]

It is not only under the palm groves of the South that these stories are a perennial delight. Wherever Buddhism has gone they have gone with it. They are known and loved on the plains of Central Asia, in the valleys of Kashmir and Afghanistan, on the cold tablelands of Nepal, Tartary and Tibet, through the vast regions of India and China, in the islands of Japan and the Malay archipelago, and throughout the jungles of Siam and Annam.

And not only so. Soldiers of Alexander who had settled in the East, wandering merchants of many nations and climes, crusading knights and hermits who had mixed with Eastern folk, brought the stories from East to West. They were very popular in Europe in the Middle Ages; and were used, more especially by the clergy, as the subjects of numerous homilies, romances, anecdotes, poems and edifying plays and mysteries. The character of the hero of them in his last or former

[1] *See* Rhys Davids' *Buddhism* (S.P.C.K.), pp. 57, 58.

births appealed so strongly to the sympathies, and especially to the religious sympathies, of mediæval Christians that the Buddha (under another name) was included, and has ever since remained, in the list of canonized saints both in the Roman and Greek Churches; and a collection of these and similar stories— wrongly but very naturally ascribed to a famous story-teller of the ancient Greeks—has become the common property, the household literature, of all the nations of Europe; and, under the name of Æsop's Fables, has handed down, as a first moral lesson-book for our children in the West, tales first invented to please and to instruct our far-off cousins in the distant East.

So the story of the migration of the stories is the most marvelous story of them all.[1] And, strange to say, in spite of the enormous out-pouring of more modern tales, these old ones have not, even yet, lost their charm. I used to tell them by the hour together, to mixed

[1] For the details of this story the introduction to my *Buddhist Birth Stories* may be consulted; and for the history of the Jâtakas in India the chapter on that subject in my *Buddhist India*.

audiences, and never found them fail. Out of
the many hundred Birth-stories there are only
a small proportion that are suitable for children. Miss Shedlock, so well known on both
sides of the Atlantic for her skill and judgment in this regard, has selected those she
deems most suitable; and, so far as I can
judge, has succeeded very admirably in adapt-
ing them for the use of children and of teachers
alike. Much depends, no doubt, upon the telling. Could Miss Shedlock herself be the teller,
there would be little doubt of the success. But
I know from my own experience that less able
story-tellers have no cause at all to be dis-
couraged.

The reason is, indeed, not far to seek. The
stories are not ordinary ones. It is not on
sharpness of repartee, or on striking incidents,
that their charm depends. These they have
sometimes. But their attraction lies rather in
a unique mixture of subtle humor, cunning
make-belief, and earnestness; in the piquancy
of the contrast between the humorous incon-
gruities and impossibilities of the details, and
the real serious earnestness, never absent but

always latent, of the ethical tone. They never raise a boisterous laugh: only a quiet smile of delighted appreciation; and they leave a pleasant aroma behind them. To the child-mind the impossibilities are no impossibilities at all, they are merely delightful. And these quaint old-world stories will continue to appeal to children, young and old, as they have done, the world over, through the long centuries of the past.

T. W. RHYS DAVIDS.

EDITOR'S PREFACE

These stories of the Buddha-Rebirths are not for one age or for one country, but for all time, and for the whole world. Their philosophy might be incorporated into the tenets of faith of a League of Nations without destroying any national forms of religious teaching. On the other hand those who prefer the foundation of more orthodox views will be astonished to find their ethics are identical with many of those inculcated in the stories: here we find condemnation of hypocrisy, cruelty, selfishness, and vice of every kind and a constant appeal to Love, Pity, Honesty, loftiness of purpose and breadth of vision. And should we reject such teachings because they were given to the World more than 2,000 years ago? Since it is wise to take into consideration the claims and interests of the passing hour it is well to re-introduce these stories at a moment when, perhaps more than ever before, East and West are struggling to arrive at a clearer understanding of one another.

In Tagore's essay on the relation of the Individual to the Universe, he says: "In the West the prevalent feeling is that Nature belongs exclusively to inanimate things and to beasts; that there is a sudden unaccountable break where human nature begins. According to it, everything that is low in the scale of beings is merely nature, and whatever has the stamp of perfection on it, intellectual or moral, is human nature. It is like dividing the bud and the blossom into two separate categories and putting their grace to the credit of two different and antithetical principles. But the Indian mind never has any hesitation in acknowledging its kinship with nature, its unbroken relation with all."

This is perhaps the best summing up of the value of this collection. Since the publication of the book in 1910, I have had many opportunities of testing the value of the dramatic appeal in these stories both for adults and boys and girls of adolescent age. When presented at this impressionable period, the inner meaning will sink more deeply into their minds than the same truths presented in a more direct and didactic fashion.

I am greatly indebted to Professor Rhys Davids, not only because he has placed the material of his translations from the Pali at my disposal, but also because of his unfailing kindness and help in directing my work. I am fortunate to have had the restraining influence of so great a scholar so that I might not lose the Indian atmosphere and line of thought which is of such value in these stories.

I most gratefully acknowledge my indebtedness to the Cambridge Press, by whose courtesy I have been able to include several of the stories published in their volumes.

I present here a selection from over 500 stories.

MARIE L. SHEDLOCK.

Cambridge, Massachusetts.

CONTENTS

INTRODUCTION

TO this new and enlarged edition of Eastern Stories and Legends, Miss Shedlock has brought years of dramatic experience in the telling of stories to children and grown people in England and America, and united with it a discriminating selection from the work of a great Oriental scholar.

The result is a book of intrinsic merit for the general reading of children and of great practical value to all who are concerned with moral or ethical training.

"I feel a great joy in what these stories can unconsciously bring to the reader," says Miss Shedlock in a personal letter, "the mere living among the stories for the past few weeks has given me a sense of calm and permanence which it is difficult to maintain under present outward conditions."

I have observed with growing interest, ex-

tending over a period of years, the effect of
such stories as "The Folly of Panic" and "The
Tree Spirit" upon audiences of adolescent
boys and girls in the public schools, public li-
braries, social settlements, Sunday schools and
private schools, I have visited with Miss Shedlock. There is in Miss Shedlock's rendering
something more than a suggestion of kinship
with Nature and the attributes of animal life.
The story is told in an atmosphere of spiritual
actuality remote from our everyday experience
yet confirming its eternal truths.

My familiarity with the earlier edition of
Eastern Stories and Legends and my personal
introduction of "The True Spirit of a Festival Day" and other stories to audiences of
parents and teachers, enables me to speak with
confidence of the value of the book in an enlarged and more popular form.

In rearranging and expanding her selection of stories Miss Shedlock has wisely freed
the book from limitations which gave it too
much the appearance of a text book. In so doing she has preserved the classical rendering
of her earlier work. Her long experience as

a teacher and story-teller in England and America informs her notes and arouses in the mature reader a fresh sense of the "power to educate" which rises out of all great literature at the touch of a true interpreter.

Annie Carroll Moore

July 14, 1920.

THE HARE THAT RAN AWAY

THE HARE THAT RAN AWAY

AND it came to pass that the Buddha (to be) was born again as a Lion. Just as he had helped his fellow-men, he now began to help his fellow-animals, and there was a great deal to be done. For instance, there was a little nervous Hare who was always afraid that something dreadful was going to happen to her. She was always saying: "Suppose the Earth were to fall in, what would happen to me?" And she said this so often that at last she thought it really was about to happen. One day, when she had been saying over and over again, "Suppose the Earth were to fall in, what would happen to me?" she heard a slight noise: it really was only a heavy fruit which had fallen upon a rustling leaf, but the little Hare was so nervous she was ready to believe anything, and she said in a frightened tone: "The Earth *is* falling in." She ran away as fast as she could go, and presently she met an

3

old brother Hare, who said: "Where are you running to, Mistress Hare?"

And the little Hare said: "I have no time to stop and tell you anything. The Earth is falling in, and I am running away."

"The Earth is falling in, is it?" said the old brother Hare, in a tone of much astonishment; and he repeated this to *his* brother hare, and *he* to *his* brother hare, and *he* to *his* brother hare, until at last there were a hundred thousand brother hares, all shouting: "The Earth is falling in." Now presently the bigger animals began to take the cry up. First the deer, and then the sheep, and then the wild boar, and then the buffalo, and then the camel, and then the tiger, and then the elephant.

Now the wise Lion heard all this noise and wondered at it. "There are no signs," he said, "of the Earth falling in. They must have heard something." And then he stopped them all short and said: "What is this you are saying?"

And the Elephant said: "I remarked that the Earth was falling in."

"How do you know this?" asked the Lion.

"Why, now I come to think of it, it was the Tiger that remarked it to me."

And the Tiger said: "*I* had it from the Camel," and the Camel said: "*I* had it from the Buffalo." And the buffalo from the wild boar, and the wild boar from the sheep, and the sheep from the deer, and the deer from the hares, and the Hares said: "Oh! *we* heard it from *that* little Hare."

And the Lion said: "Little Hare, *what* made you say that the Earth was falling in?"

And the little Hare said: "I *saw* it."

"You saw it?" said the Lion. "Where?"

"Yonder, by the tree."

"Well," said the Lion, "come with me and I will show you how——"

"No, no," said the Hare, "I would not go near that tree for anything, I'm *so* nervous."

"But," said the Lion, "I am going to take you on my back." And he took her on his back, and begged the animals to stay where they were until they returned. Then he showed the little Hare how the fruit had fallen upon the leaf, making the noise that had frightened her, and she said: "Yes, I see—the

Earth is *not* falling in." And the Lion said: "Shall we go back and tell the other animals?" And they went back. The little Hare stood before the animals and said: "The Earth is *not* falling in." And all the animals began to repeat this to one another, and they dispersed gradually, and you heard the words more and more softly:

"The Earth is *not* falling in," etc., etc., etc., until the sound died away altogether.

Note.—This story I have told in my own words, using the language I have found most effective for very young children.

THE MONKEY AND THE CROCODILE

THE MONKEY AND THE CROCODILE

ONCE upon a time, while Brahmadatta was king of Benares, the Bodhisatta came to life at the foot of Himalaya as a Monkey. He grew strong and sturdy, big of frame, well-to-do, and lived by a curve of the river Ganges in a forest haunt.

Now at that time there was a Crocodile dwelling in the Ganges. The Crocodile's mate saw the great frame of the monkey, and she conceived a longing for his heart to eat. So she said to her lord: "Sir, I desire to eat the heart of that great king of the monkeys!"

"Good wife," said the Crocodile, "I live in the water and he lives on dry land: how can we catch him?"

"By hook or by crook," she replied, "caught he must be. If I don't get him, I shall die."

"All right," answered the Crocodile, con-

soling her, "don't trouble yourself. I have a
plan; I will give you his heart to eat."

So when the Bodhisatta was sitting on the
bank of the Ganges, after taking a drink of
water, the Crocodile drew near, and said:

"Sir Monkey, why do you live on bad fruits
in this old familiar place? On the other side
of the Ganges there is no end to the mango
trees, and labuja trees, with fruit sweet as
honey! Is it not better to cross over and have
all kinds of wild fruit to eat?"

"Lord Crocodile," the Monkey made answer, "deep and wide is the Ganges: how shall
I get across?"

"If you will go, I will mount you on my
back, and carry you over."

The Monkey trusted him, and agreed.
"Come here, then," said the other, "up on my
back with you!" and up the Monkey climbed.
But when the Crocodile had swum a little way,
he plunged the Monkey under the water.

"Good friend, you are letting me sink!" cried
the Monkey. "What is that for?"

Said the Crocodile, "You think I am carrying you out of pure good nature? Not a bit of

it! My wife has a longing for your heart, and I want to give it to her to eat!"

"Friend," said the Monkey, "it is nice of you to tell me. Why, if our heart were inside us when we go jumping among the tree-tops, it would be all knocked to pieces!"

"Well, where do you keep it?" asked the other.

The Bodhisatta pointed out a fig-tree, with clusters of ripe fruit, standing not far off. "See," said he, "there are our hearts hanging on yon fig-tree."

"If you will show me your heart," said the Crocodile, "then I won't kill you."

"Take me to the tree, then, and I will point it out to you hanging upon it."

The Crocodile brought him to the place. The Monkey leapt off his back, and climbing up the fig-tree sat upon it. "O silly Crocodile!" said he, "you thought that there were creatures that kept their hearts in a tree-top! You are a fool, and I have outwitted you! You may keep your fruit to yourself. Your body is great, but you have no sense." And then to explain this idea he uttered the following stanzas:

"Rose-apple, jack-fruit, mangoes too across
the water there I see;
Enough of them, I want them not; my fig is
good enough for me!

"Great is your body, verily, but how much
smaller is your wit!
Now go your ways, Sir Crocodile, for I have
had the best of it."

The Crocodile, feeling as sad and miserable
as if he had lost a thousand pieces of money,
went back sorrowing to the place where he
lived.

THE SPIRIT THAT LIVED
IN A TREE

THE SPIRIT THAT LIVED
IN A TREE

A ND it came to pass that the Buddha was re-born as a Tree-Spirit. Now there reigned (at Benares) at that time a King who said to himself: "All over India, the kings live in palaces supported by many a column. *I* will build me a palace resting on one column only —then shall I in truth be the chiefest of all kings."

Now in the King's Park was a lordly Sal tree, straight and well-grown, worshiped by village and town, and to this tree even the Royal Family also paid tribute, worship, and honor. And then suddenly there came an order from the King that the tree should be cut down.

And the people were sore dismayed, but the woodmen, who dared not disobey the orders of the King, came to the Park with hands full of perfumed garlands, and encircling the tree with a string, fastened to it a nosegay of flowers, and kindling a lamp, they did worship, exclaiming: "O Tree! on the seventh day must we cut thee down, for so hath the King commanded. Now let the Deities who dwell within thee go elsewhither, and since we are only obeying the King's command, let no blame fall upon us, and no harm come to our children because of this."

And the Spirit who lived in the tree, hearing these words, reflected within himself and said: "These builders are determined to cut down this tree, and to destroy my place of dwelling. Now my life lasts only as long as this tree. And lo! all the young Sal trees that stand around, where dwell the Deities my kinsfolk—and they are many—will be destroyed! My own destruction does not touch me so near as the destruction of my children: therefore must I protect their lives."

Accordingly, at the hour of midnight adorned in divine splendor, he entered into the magnificent chamber of the King, and filling the whole chamber with a bright radiance, stood weeping beside the King's pillow. At the sight of him, the King, overcome with terror, said: "Who art thou, standing high in the air, and why do thy tears flow?"

And the Tree-God made answer: "Within thy realm I am known as the Lucky-Tree. For sixty thousand years have I stood, and all have worshiped me, and though they have built many a house, and many a town, no violence has been done to me. Spare thou me, also, O King."

Then the King made answer and said: "Never have I seen so mighty a trunk, so thick and strong a tree; but I will build me a palace, and thou shalt be the only column on which it shall rest, and thou shalt dwell there for ever."

And the Tree said: "Since thou art resolved to tear my body from me, I pray thee cut me down gently, one branch after another—the root last of all."

And the King said: "O Woodland Tree! what is this thou askest of me? It were a painful death to die. One stroke at the root would fell thee to the ground. Why wouldst thou die piecemeal?"

And the Tree made answer: "O King! My children, the young Sal trees, all grow at my feet: they are prosperous and well sheltered. If I should fall with one mighty crash, behold these young children of the forest would perish also!"

And the King was greatly moved by this spirit of sacrifice, and said: "O great and glorious Tree! I set thee free from thy fear, and because thou wouldst willingly die to save thy kindred, thou shalt not be cut down. Return to thy home in the Ancient Forest."

THE HARE THAT WAS NOT
AFRAID TO DIE

THE HARE THAT WAS NOT
AFRAID TO DIE

A ND it came to pass that the Buddha was
born a Hare and lived in a wood; on one
side was the foot of a mountain, on another
a river, on the third side a border village.

And with him lived three friends: a Monkey, a Jackal, and an Otter; each of these
creatures got food on his own hunting ground.
In the evening they met together, and the
Hare taught his companions many wise things:
that the moral law should be observed—that
alms should be given to the poor, and that
holy days should be kept.

One day the Buddha said: "To-morrow is
a fast day. Feed any beggars that come to
you by giving from your own store of food."
They all consented.

The next day the Otter went down to the
bank of the Ganges to seek his prey. Now
a fisherman had landed seven red fish and had

buried them in the sand on the river's bank while he went down the stream catching more. The Otter scented the buried fish, dug up the sand till he came upon them, and he called aloud: "Does any one own these fish?" And, not seeing the owner, he laid the fish in the jungle where he dwelt, intending to eat them at a fitting time. Then he lay down, thinking how virtuous he was.

The Jackal also went off in search of food, and found in the hut of a field watcher a lizard, and a pot of milk-curd.

And, after thrice crying aloud, "To whom do these belong?" and not finding an owner, he put on his neck the rope for lifting the pot, and grasping the spits and lizard with his teeth, he laid them in his own lair, thinking, "In due season I will devour them," and then he lay down, thinking how virtuous he had been.

The Monkey entered the clump of trees, and gathering a bunch of mangoes, laid them up in his part of the jungle, meaning to eat them in due season. He then lay down and thought how virtuous he had been.

But the Hare (who was the Buddha-to-be) in due time came out thinking to lie (in contemplation) on the Kuca grass. "It is impossible for me to offer *grass* to any beggars who may chance to come by, and I have no oil or rice or fish. If any beggar come to me, I will give him (of) my own flesh to eat."

Now when Sakka, the King of the Gods, heard this thing, he determined to put the Royal Hare to the test. So he came in disguise of a Brahmin to the Otter and said: "Wise Sir, if I could get something to eat, I would perform *all* my priestly duties."

The Otter said: "I will give you food. Seven red fish have I safely brought to land from the sacred river of the Ganges. Eat thy fill, O Brahmin, and stay in this wood."

And the Brahmin said: "Let it be until tomorrow, and I will see to it then."

Then he went to the Jackal, who confessed that he had stolen the food, but he begged the Brahmin to accept it and remain in the wood; but the Brahmin said: "Let it be until tomorrow, and then I will see to it."

And he came to the Monkey, who offered

him the mangoes, and the Brahmin answered in the same way.

Then the Brahmin went to the wise Hare, and the Hare said: "Behold, I will give thee of my flesh to eat. But thou must not take life on this holy day. When thou hast piled up the logs I will sacrifice myself by falling into the midst of the flames, and when my body is roasted thou shalt eat it and perform all thy priestly duties."

Now when Sakka heard these words he caused a heap of burning coals to appear, and the Wisdom Being, rising from the grass, came to the place, but before casting himself into the flames he shook himself, lest perchance there should be any insects in his coat who might suffer death. Then, offering his body as a free gift, he sprang up, and like a royal swan, lighting on a bed of lotus in an ecstasy of joy, he fell on the heap of live coals. But the flame failed even to heat the pores of the hair on the body of the Wisdom Being, and it was as if he had entered a region of frost. Then he addressed the Brahmin in these words: "Brahmin, the fire that thou hast kindled is icy cold; it fails to heat the pores of the hair on my body. What is the meaning of this?"

"O most wise Hare! I am Sakka, and have come to put your virtue to the test."

And the Buddha in a sweet voice said: "No god or man could find in me an unwillingness to die."

Then Sakka said: "O wise Hare, be thy virtue known to all the ages to come." '

And seizing the mountain he squeezed out the juice and daubed on the moon the signs of the young hare.

Then he placed him back on the grass that he might continue his Sabbath meditation and returned to Heaven.

And the four creatures lived together and kept the moral law.

THE PARROT THAT FED HIS PARENTS

THE PARROT THAT FED HIS PARENTS

NOW it came to pass that the Buddha was re-born in the shape of a Parrot, and he greatly excelled all other parrots in his strength and beauty. And when he was full grown his father, who had long been the leader of the flock in their flights to other climes, said to him: "My son, behold my strength is spent! Do thou lead the flock, for I am no longer able." And the Buddha said: "Behold, thou shalt rest. I will lead the birds." And the Parrots rejoiced in the strength of their new leader, and willingly did they follow him. Now from that day on, the Buddha undertook to feed his parents, and would not consent that they should do any more work. Each day he led his flock to the Himalaya Hills, and when he had eaten his fill of the clumps of rice that grew there, he filled his beak with food for the dear parents who were waiting his return.

Now there was a man appointed to watch the rice-fields, and he did his best to drive the Parrots away, but there seemed to be some secret power in the leader of this flock which the Keeper could not overcome.

He noticed that the Parrots ate their fill and then flew away, but that the Parrot-King not only satisfied his hunger, but carried away rice in his beak.

Now he feared there would be no rice left, and he went to his master the Brahmin to tell him what had happened; and even as the master listened there came to him the thought that the Parrot-King was something higher than he seemed, and he loved him even before he saw him. But he said nothing of this, and only warned the Keeper that he should set a snare and catch the dangerous bird. So the man did as he was bidden: he made a small cage and set the snare, and sat down in his hut waiting for the birds to come. And soon he saw the Parrot-King amidst his flock, who, because he had no greed, sought no richer spot, but flew down to the same place in which he had fed the day before.

Now, no sooner had he touched the ground than he felt his feet caught in the noose. Then fear crept into his bird-heart, but a stronger feeling was there to crush it down, for he thought: "If I cry out the Cry of the Captured, my Kinsfolk will be terrified, and they will fly away foodless. But if I lie still, then their hunger will be satisfied, and they may safely come to my aid." Thus was the Parrot both brave and prudent.

But alas! he did not know that his Kinsfolk had nought of his brave spirit. When *they* had eaten their fill, though they heard the thrice-uttered cry of the captured, they flew away, nor heeded the sad plight of their leader.

Then was the heart of the Parrot-King sore within him, and he said: "All these my kith and kin, and not one to look back on me. Alas! what sin have I done?"

The Watchman now heard the cry of the Parrot-King, and the sound of the other Parrots flying through the air. "What is that?" he cried, and leaving his hut he came to the place where he had laid the snare. There he found the captive Parrot; he tied his feet together and brought him to the Brahmin, his master. Now, when the Brahmin saw the Parrot-King, he felt his strong power, and his heart was full of love to him, but he hid his feelings and said in a voice of anger: "Is thy greed greater than that of all other birds? They eat their fill, but thou takest away each day more food than thou canst eat. Doest thou this out of hatred for me, or dost thou store up the food in some granary for selfish greed?"

And the Great Being made answer in a sweet human voice: "I hate thee not, O Brahmin. Nor do I store the rice in a granary for selfish greed. But this thing I do. Each day I pay a debt which is due—each day I grant a loan, and each day I store up a treasure."

Now the Brahmin could not understand the words of the Buddha (because true wisdom had not entered his heart), and he said: "I pray thee, O Wondrous Bird, to make these words clear unto me."

And then the Parrot-King made answer: "I carry food to my ancient parents who can no longer seek that food for themselves:

thus I pay my daily debt. I carry food to my callow chicks whose wings are yet ungrown. When I am old they will care for me —this my loan to them. And for other birds, weak and helpless of wing, who need the aid of the strong, for them I lay up a store; to these I give in charity."

Then was the Brahmin much moved, and showed the love that was in his heart. "Eat thy fill, O Righteous Bird, and let thy Kinsfolk eat too, for thy sake." And he wished to bestow a thousand acres of land upon him, but the Great Being would only take a tiny portion round which were set boundary stores.

And the Parrot returned with a head of rice, and said: "Arise, dear Parents, that I may take you to a place of plenty." And he told them the story of his deliverance.

THE MAN WHO WORKED TO GIVE ALMS

THE MAN WHO WORKED TO
GIVE ALMS

ONCE upon a time the Buddha was born as a merchant named Vissaya (and being endowed with the Five Virtues) he was liberal and fond of alms-giving. He had alms halls built at the four city gates, in the heart of the city, and at the door of his own house. At these points he set on foot alms-giving and every day 600,000 men went forth to beg and the food of the beggar and the merchant was exactly the same. And as he thus stirred up the people of India by his gifts, Sakka, the King of the gods, grew suspicious and thought, "This Vissaya gives alms and by scattering his gifts everywhere is stirring up all India. By means of his alms-giving, methinks he will dethrone me and himself become Sakka. I will destroy his wealth, and make him a poor man, and so bring it about that he shall no longer give alms." So Sakka caused his oil, honey, molasses and the like, and all his treasure of grain to disappear, as well as his slaves and work people. Those who were deprived of his gifts came and said, "My Lord, the alms hall has disappeared. We do not find anything in the various places set up by you." "Take money hence," he said. "Do not cut off the giving of alms." And calling his wife, he bade her keep up her charity. She searched the whole house, and not finding a single bit of money, she said, "My Lord, except the clothes we wear, I see nothing. The whole house is empty." Opening the seven jewel treasuries they found nothing, and save the merchant and his wife no one else was seen, neither slaves nor hirelings. The merchant, again addressing his wife, said, "My dear, we cannot possibly cut off our charities. Search the whole house till you find something."

At that moment a certain grass-mower threw down his sickle and pole and the rope for binding the grass in the doorway, and ran away. The merchant's wife found them and said: "My Lord, this is all I see," and brought and gave them to him. Said he: "All these years I have never mown grass before, but to-day I will mow grass, and take and sell it, and by this means dispense the fitting alms."

So, through fear of having to cut off his charities, he took the sickle, and the pole and the rope, and going forth from the city came to a place of much grass, and mowing it, tied it up in two bundles, saying, "One shall belong to us, and with the other I will give alms."

This he did for six days, and because there was not enough to feed all who came for alms, on the seventh day, he and his wife went fasting. Then his strength gave out. No sooner did the heat of the sun strike upon his head than his eyes began to swim in his head, and he became unconscious, and falling down he scattered the grass. Sakka was moving about, observing what the merchant did. And that god, standing in mid-air, cried: "Refrain from giving, and thou shalt have joy for ever."

"Who art thou?" cried the merchant.

"I am Sakka."

And the merchant said:

"Sakka reached his high office by taking upon himself moral duties, and giving alms."

"Why dost thou give alms?" asked Sakka, still wishing to test him.

"It is not because I desire Sakkahood nor Brahmaship, but through giving there cometh knowledge of all things."

"Great merchant," cried Sakka, "henceforth do thou every day give alms." And all his wealth was restored to him.

THE KING WHO SAW THE TRUTH

THE KING WHO SAW THE TRUTH

LONG, long ago the Wisdom Child that should in time become the Buddha was born a King. He was kind and generous, distributing all sorts of alms to the poor; nor did he leave the work to those under him: he took a personal part in the giving of the gifts —and nearly every day came himself to the Alms Hall to see that none went away empty-handed.

But one morning, as he lay meditating on what he still might do for his people, he began to feel that, after all, he had done no very great thing, and he said: "I have given to my people only *outside* things—the mere gold and silver and raiment and food that I can well spare, and lo! this giving brings me no joy. If I could only give my people part of myself—some precious thing which would show my love for them—whatever it might cost me! And if to-day, when I go down to

43

the Alms Hall, one should say, 'Give me thy
heart,' then, in truth, I will cut open my breast
with a spear, and, as though I were drawing
up a water-lily from a calm lake, I will pull
forth my heart. If he asks my flesh and blood,
behold I will give it to him. If he complain
that there is no other to do his work, then I
will leave my royal throne, and, proclaiming
myself a slave, I will do the work of a slave—
and, indeed, should any man ask for my eyes,
the most precious gift of the gods, then will I
tear them out as one might tear the pith from
the palm-tree."

Then he bathed himself, and, mounted upon
a richly caparisoned elephant, he rode down
to the Alms Hall, his heart filled with love
for his people.

Now Sakka, the King of the Gods, heard
the resolve of the King, and he thought to
test him, whether his words were vain; whether
it were a sudden mood which would pass away
when the moment came to carry out his stern
resolution.

So, when the King came down to the Alms
Hall, Sakka stood before him, in the guise of

an old blind Brahmin, who, stretching out his hands, cried out: "Long live the King!"

And the King made sign for him to say what was in his heart.

"O great King," said the blind Brahmin— "in all the inhabited world there is no spot where the fame of thy great heart has not spread. I am blind, but thou, O King, hast *two* eyes—I therefore beseech thee, give me *one,* that I too may behold the glories of the Earth!"

Then did the King rejoice greatly that this opportunity should have come to him so quickly, but not wishing to show at once the joy he felt in his heart, he said: "O Brahmin, I pray thee tell me, who bade thee wend thy way to this alms-house? Thou askest of me the most precious thing that a man possesses, and lo! it is very hard to give!"

And the Brahmin made answer: "Behold, a god has sent me hither, and has told me to ask this boon."

And the King said: "Thy prayer is granted: thou didst ask for one eye, behold I will give thee both eyes."

And then the news spread quickly through the town that the King was about to give his eyes to a blind Brahmin, and the Commander-in-Chief and all the officials gathered together that they might turn the King from his purpose.

And they said: "O great King, are there not other gifts which thou canst bestow upon this sightless Brahmin—money, jewels, elephants with cloth of gold? Why shouldst thou give to him that most precious of gifts, thy royal eyes?"

And the King said: "Behold, I have taken this vow, and I should be sinful if I were to break it."

And the courtiers said: "O King, why doest thou this thing? Is it for Life, or Beauty or Strength?"

The King answered: "It is for none of these things: it is for the joy of giving."

Then the King bid the Surgeon do his work. And when one of his eyes was taken out, he gave it to the Brahmin, and it remained fixed in his socket like a blue lotus flower in bloom. And the King said: "The eye that sees all things is greater than this eye," and, being filled with ecstasy of joy, he gave the second eye.

And after many days and much suffering, the King's sight was restored to him—not the natural eyes which see the things around—but the eyes which see perfect and absolute Truth.

And he reigned in righteousness and justice, and the people learnt of him pure wisdom.

THE BULL THAT DEMANDED
FAIR TREATMENT

THE BULL THAT DEMANDED FAIR TREATMENT

LONG ago the Bodisat came to life as a Bull.

Now, when he was yet a young calf, a certain Brahmin, after attending upon some devotees who were wont to give oxen to priests, received the bull. And he called it Nandi Visāla, and grew very fond of it, treating it like a son, and feeding it on gruel and rice.

When the Bodisat grew up, he said to himself: "This Brahmin has brought me up with great care; and there's no other ox in all the continent of India can drag the weight I can. What if I were to let the Brahmin know about my strength, and so in my turn provide sustenance for him!"

And he said one day to the Brahmin: "Do you go now, Brahmin, to some Squire rich in cattle, and offer to bet him a thousand that your ox will move a hundred laden carts."

The Brahmin went to a rich farmer, and started a conversation thus:

"Whose bullocks hereabout do you think the strongest?"

"Such and such a man's," said the farmer, and then added: "But, of course, there are none in the whole country-side to touch my own!"

"I have one ox," said the Brahmin, "who is good to move a hundred carts, loads and all!"

"Tush!" said the Squire. "Where in the world is such an ox?"

"Just in my house!" said the Brahmin.

"Then make a bet about it!"

"All right! I bet you a thousand he can."

So the bet was made. And he filled a hundred carts (small wagons made for two bullocks) with sand and gravel and stones, ranged them all in a row, and tied them all firmly together, cross-bar to axle-tree.

Then he bathed Nandi Visāla, gave him a measure of scented rice, hung a garland round his neck, and yoked him by himself to the front cart. Then he took his seat on the pole, raised his goad aloft, and called out: "Gee up! you brute!! Drag 'em along, you wretch!!"

The Bodisat said to himself: "He addresses me as a wretch. I am no wretch!" And, keeping his four legs as firm as so many posts, he stood perfectly still.

Then the Squire that moment claimed his bet, and made the Brahmin hand over the thousand pieces. And the Brahmin, minus his thousand, took out his ox, went home to his house, and lay down overwhelmed with grief.

Presently Nandi Visāla, who was roaming about the place, came up and saw the Brahmin grieving there, and said to him: "What, Brahmin! Are you asleep?"

"Sleep! How can I sleep after losing the thousand pieces?"

"Brahmin! I've lived so long in your house, and have I ever broken any pots, or rubbed up against the walls?"

"Never, my dear!"

"Then why did you call me a wretch? It's your fault. It's not my fault. Go now and bet him two thousand; and never call me a wretch again—I, who am no wretch at all!"

When the Brahmin heard what he said, he made the bet two thousand, tied the carts together as before, decked out Nandi Visāla, and yoked him to the foremost cart.

He managed this in the following way: he tied the pole and the cross-piece fast together, yoked Nandi Visāla on one side; on the other he fixed a smooth piece of timber from the point of the yoke to the axle-end, and wrapping it round with the fastenings of the cross-piece, tied it fast, so that when this was done the yoke could not move this way and that way, and it was possible for one ox to drag forwards the double bullock-cart.

Then the Brahmin seated himself on the pole, stroked Nandi Visāla on the back, and called out: "Gee up! my beauty!! Drag it along, my beauty!!"

And the Bodisat, with one mighty effort, dragged forwards the hundred heavily-laden carts, and brought the hindmost one up to the place where the foremost one had stood.

Then the cattle-owner acknowledged himself beaten, and handed over to the Brahmin the two thousand; the bystanders, too, presented the Bodisat with a large sum, and the whole became the property of the Brahmin. Thus, by means of the Bodisat, great was the wealth he acquired.

THE BULL THAT PROVED
HIS GRATITUDE

THE BULL THAT PROVED
HIS GRATITUDE

L ONG ago . . . the Bodisat returned to
life as a Bull.

Now, when it was still a young calf, its
owners stopped a while in an old woman's
house, and gave him to her when they settled
their account for their lodging. And she
brought him up, treating him like a son, and
feeding him on gruel and rice.

He soon became known as "The old woman's
Blackie." When he grew up, he roamed about,
as black as collyrium, with the village cattle,
and was very good-tempered and quiet. The
village children used to catch hold of his horns,
or ears, or dewlaps, and hang on to him; or
amuse themselves by pulling his tail, or riding
about on his back.

One day he said to himself: "My mother
is wretchedly poor. She's taken so much pains,
too, in bringing me up, and has treated me like

a son. What if I were to work for hire, and
so relieve her distress!" And from that day
he was always on the look-out for a job.

Now, one day a young caravan owner arrived at a neighboring ford with five hundred
bullock-wagons. And his bullocks were not
only unable to drag the carts across, but
even when he yoked the five hundred pair in
a row they could not move one cart by itself.

The Bodisat was grazing with the village
cattle close to the ford. The young caravan
owner was a famous judge of cattle, and
began looking about to see whether there were
among them any thoroughbred bull able to
drag over the carts. Seeing the Bodisat, he
thought he would do, and asked the herdsmen:
"Who may be the owners, my men, of this
fellow? I should like to yoke him to the cart,
and am willing to give a reward for having the
carts dragged over."

"Catch him and yoke him then," said they.
"He has no owner hereabouts."

But when he began to put a string through
his nose and drag him along, he could not get
him to come. For the Bodisat, it is said,

wouldn't go till he was promised a reward.

The young caravan owner, seeing what his object was, said to him: "Sir! if you'll drag over these five hundred carts for me, I'll pay you wages at the rate of two pence for each cart—a thousand pieces in all."

Then the Bodisat went along of his own accord, and the men yoked him to the cart. And with a mighty effort he dragged it up and landed it safe on the high ground. And in the same manner he dragged up all the carts.

So the caravan owner then put five hundred pennies in a bundle, one for each cart, and tied it round his neck. The Bull said to himself: "This fellow is not giving me wages according to the rate agreed upon. I shan't let him go on now!" And so he went and stood in the way of the front cart, and they tried in vain to get him away.

The caravan owner thought: "He knows, I suppose, that the pay is too little;" and wrapping a thousand pieces in a cloth, tied them up in a bundle, and hung that round his neck. And as soon as he got the bundle with a thousand inside, he went off to his "mother."

Then the village children called out: "See! what's that round the neck of the old woman's Blackie?" and began to run up to him. But he chased after them, so that they took to their heels before they got near him; and he went straight to his "mother." And he appeared with eyes all bloodshot, utterly exhausted from dragging over so many carts.

"How did you get this, dear?" said the good old woman, when she saw the bag round his neck. And when she heard, on inquiry from the herdsmen, what had happened, she exclaimed: "Am I so anxious, then, to live on the fruit of your toil, my darling! Why do you put yourself to all this pain?"

And she bathed him in warm water, and rubbed him all over with oil, and gave him to drink, and fed him up with good food. And at the end of her life she passed away according to her deeds, and the Bodisat with her.

THE HORSE THAT HELD
OUT TO THE END

THE HORSE THAT HELD
OUT TO THE END

A ND it came to pass that the Buddha (to
be) came to life in the shape of a Horse
—a thoroughbred small horse, and he was
made the King's Destrier, surrounded by
pomp and state. He was fed on exquisite
three-year-old rice which was always served up
to him in a golden dish worth a hundred thousand pieces of money, and the ground of his
stall was perfumed with the four odors. Round
his stall were hung crimson curtains, while
overhead was a canopy studded with stars of
gold. On the wall were festooned wreaths and
garlands of fragrant flowers, and a lamp fed
with scented oil was always burning there.

Now all the kings round coveted the kingdom of Benares. Once seven kings passed
Benares and sent a missive to the King, saying:
"Either yield up your kingdom to us or give
battle."

Assembling his ministers, the King of Benares laid the matter before them and asked what he was to do. Said they: "You ought not to go out to battle in person, Sire, in the first instance. Despatch such and such a Knight out first to fight him, and, later on, if he fall, we will decide what to do."

Then the King sent for that Knight and said to him: "Can you fight the seven kings, my dear Knight?" Said he: "Give me but your noble Destrier, and then I could fight not only seven kings but all the kings in India." "My dear Knight, take my Destrier or any horse you please, and do battle." "Very good, my Sovereign Lord," said the Knight, and with a bow he passed down from the upper chambers of the palace.

Then he had the noble Destrier led out and sheathed in mail, arming himself too and girding on his sword.

Mounted on his noble steed he passed out of the City Gate, and with a lightning charge broke down the first camp, taking one king alone, and bringing him back a prisoner to the soldiers' custody.

. . . And this went on until six kings had been made prisoner. Then the noble Horse received a wound which streamed with blood and caused him much pain. Perceiving that the Horse was wounded, the Knight made it lie down at the King's gate, loosened its mail, and set about arming another horse.

But the Horse perceiving this, said: "The other horse will *not* be able to break down the seventh camp and capture the seventh king: he will lose all that I have accomplished. The peerless Knight will be slain, and the King will fall into the hands of the foe. I alone and no other horse can break down the seventh camp and capture the seventh king."

So he called to the Knight and repeated these words, and added: "I will not throw away what I have already done. Only have me set upon my feet, and clad again in my armor, and I will accomplish my work."

The Knight had the Horse set upon his feet, bound up his wound, and armed him again in proof. Mounted on the Destrier, he broke down the seventh camp, and brought back alive the seventh king.

They led the Horse to the King's gate, and the King came up to look at him.

Then said the Great Being: "Great King, slay not these seven kings: bind them by an oath, and let them go. Let the Knight enjoy the honor due to us both. As for you, exercise charity, keep the Ornaments, and rule your kingdom in righteousness and justice." When the Horse had thus exhorted the King, they took off his mail, but as they were taking it off piecemeal, he passed away.

The King had the body buried with due respect, bestowed great honors on the Knight, and sent the kings to their homes, after exacting from each an oath never to war upon him any more. And he ruled his kingdom in righteousness and justice, passing away when his life closed, to fare thereafter according to his deserts.

The story was told by the Master about a brother who gave up persevering.

"Brethren, in bygone days the wise and good persevered even in hostile surroundings, and even when they were wounded they did not give in. Whereas you who have devoted yourself to so saving a doctrine, how comes it that you give up persevering?"

THE MONKEY THAT SAVED
THE HERD

THE MONKEY THAT SAVED
THE HERD

IT came to pass that the Buddha was re-born as the King of the monkeys. He lived with his herd of 80,000 monkeys in a thick forest, near a lake. In this lake there lived an ogre who used to devour all those who went down to the water.

The Buddha spoke to his subjects and said: "My friends, in this forest there are trees that are poisoned, and lakes that are haunted by ogres. Eat no fruit and drink no water of which you have not already tasted without consulting me."

This they agreed to. And one day, having arrived at a spot which they had never visited before, they found a great lake. They did not drink, but awaited the return of their King.

Now when he arrived he went round the

lake, and found that all the footsteps led down
to the lake, but none came up again. And
he said: "Without doubt this is the haunt of
an ogre."

When this water-ogre saw that they were
not invading his domain he appeared in the
form of a terrible monster with a blue belly,
a white face, and bright red hands and feet.
In this shape he came out of the water and
said to the King: "Why are you seated here?
Go down to the lake to drink." But the King
said: "Are you not the ogre of this water?"
"Yes, I am," was the answer. "Do you take
as your prey all those who go down into this
water?" "Yes, I do, from small birds up-
wards. I never let anything go which comes
down into this water. I will eat the lot of you,
too." "But we shall not let you eat us." "Just
drink the water." "Yes, we will drink the
water, and yet not fall into your power."
"How do you propose to drink the water,
then?" "Ah, you think we shall have to go
down to the water to drink; whereas we shall
not enter the water at all, but the whole eighty

thousand of us will take a cane each and drink therewith from your lake as easily as through the hollow stalk of a lotus. And so you will not be able to eat us."

So saying the King had a cane brought to him, and in true belief that the miracle would take place he blew down the cane, which straightway became hollow throughout, without a single knot being left in its length. In this fashion he had another, and another brought, and blew down them. Then he made the tour of the lake, and commanded, saying, "Let all canes growing here become hollow throughout." Now, thanks to the saving goodness of their re-born chiefs, their commands are always fulfilled. And henceforth every single cane that grew round that lake became hollow throughout. After giving his commands the King seated himself with a cane in his hand. All the other 80,000 monkeys, too, seated themselves round the lake each with a cane in his hands. At the same moment when the King sucked up the water through his cane, they all drank in the same manner as they sat on the bank. This was the way they drank, and the ogre could get no power over any one of them, so he went off in a rage to his habitation. The King, with his following of 80,000 monkeys, went back into the forest.

THE MALLARD THAT ASKED
FOR TOO MUCH

THE MALLARD THAT ASKED
FOR TOO MUCH

AND it came to pass that the Buddha (to be) was born a Brahmin, and growing up was married to a bride of his own rank, who bore him three daughters.

After his death he was born again as a Golden Mallard, and he determined to give his golden feathers one at a time to enable his wife and daughters to live in comfort. So away he flew to where they dwelt, and alighted on the central beam of the roof.

Seeing the Bodisat, the wife and girls asked where he had come from, and he told them that he was their father who had died and been born a Golden Mallard, and that he had come to bring them help. "You shall have my golden feathers, one by one," he said. He gave them one and departed. From time to time he returned to give them another feather, and they became quite wealthy.

But one day the mother said: "There's no trusting animals, my children. Who's to say your father might not go away one of these days and never return? Let us use our time, and pluck him clean the next time he comes, so as to make sure of all his feathers." Thinking this would pain him, the daughters refused. The mother in her greed·plucked the Mallard herself, and as she plucked them against his wish, they ceased to be golden and became like a crane's feathers. His wings grew again, but they were plain white; he flew away to his own abode and never came back.

THE MERCHANT WHO OVER-CAME ALL OBSTACLES

THE MERCHANT WHO OVER-
CAME ALL OBSTACLES

ONCE upon a time the Buddha (to be) was born in a merchant's family; and when he grew up he went about trafficking with five hundred carts.

One day he arrived at a sandy desert twenty leagues across. The sand in that desert was so fine that when taken in the closed fist it could not be kept in the hand. After the sun had risen it became as hot as a mass of charcoal, so that no man could walk on it. Those, therefore, who had to travel over it took wood and water and oil and rice in their carts, and traveled during the night. And at daybreak they formed an encampment, and spread an awning over it, and, taking their meals early, they passed the day sitting in the shade. At sunset they supped; and when the ground had become cool, they yoked their oxen and went on. The traveling was like a voyage over the sea: a so-called land-pilot had to be chosen, and he brought the caravan safe to the other side by his knowledge of the stars.

On this occasion the merchant of our story traversed the desert in that way. And when he had passed over fifty-nine leagues, he thought: "Now in one more night we shall get out of the sand." And after supper he directed the wood and water to be thrown away, and the wagons to be yoked, and so set out. The pilot had cushions arranged on the foremost cart, and lay down looking at the stars, and directing them where to drive. But, worn out by want of rest during the long march, he fell asleep, and did not perceive that the oxen had turned around and taken the same road by which they had come.

The oxen went on the whole night through. Towards dawn the pilot woke up, and, observing the stars, called out: "Stop the wagons! Stop the wagons!" The day broke just as they had stopped, and were drawing up the carts in a line. Then the men cried out: "Why, this is the very encampment we left yesterday! Our wood and water is all gone! We are lost!"

And unyoking the oxen, and spreading the canopy over their heads, they lay down in despondency, each one under his wagon.

But the Bodisat, saying to himself, "If I lose heart, all these will perish," walked about while the morning was yet cool. And on seeing a tuft of Kusa grass, he thought: "This must have grown by attracting some water which there must be beneath it."

And he made them bring a hoe and dig in that spot. And they dug sixty cubits deep. And when they had got thus far, the spade of the diggers struck on a rock, and as soon as it struck, they all gave up in despair.

But the Bodisat thought, "There must be water under that rock," and, stooping down, applied his ear to it and tested the sound of it. And he heard the sound of water gurgling beneath. And he got out and called his page. "My lad, if you give up now, we shall all be lost. Don't you lose heart. Take this iron hammer, and go down into the pit and give the rock a good blow."

The lad obeyed, and though they all stood by in despair, he went down full of determina-

tion, and struck at the stone. And the rock
split in two and fell below, and no longer
blocked up the stream. And water rose till
its brim was the height of a palm-tree in the
well. And they all drank of the water, and
bathed in it. Then they split up their extra
yokes and axles, and cooked rice and ate it,
and fed their oxen with it. And when the sun
set, they put up a flag by the well and went
to the place appointed. There they sold their
merchandise at double and treble profit, and
returned to their own home, and lived to a
good old age, and then passed away according
to their deeds. And the Bodisat gave gifts,
and did other virtuous acts, and passed away
according to his deeds.

THE ELEPHANT THAT WAS
HONORED IN OLD AGE

THE ELEPHANT THAT WAS
HONORED IN OLD AGE

A ND the Buddha as Prime Minister served
the King. Now there was a certain She-
Elephant endowed with great might which
enabled her to go a hundred leagues a day.
She did the duties of messenger to the King,
and in battle she fought and crushed the
enemy. The King said: "She is very service-
able to me."

He gave her ornaments, and caused all
honor to be shown her. Then, when she was
weak from age, the King took away all the
honor he had bestowed.

From that time she was unprotected, and
lived by eating grass and leaves in the forest.

And one day the chief Potter had not
enough oxen to yoke to the carts which carried the material for making clay. And the
King said: "Where is our She-Elephant?"

"O King! she is wandering at her will in the forest."

And the King said: "Do thou yoke her to the cart."

And the Potter said: " Good, O King!" And he did even as the King commanded.

But when this insult was offered to the Elephant, she came to the Prime Minister and said: "O Wise Being! I pray you listen to my tale. When I was young, great strength was mine; and I did walk a hundred leagues to bear the King's messages, and, with weapons bound upon my body, I did take part in battle, crushing the enemy beneath my feet. And now I am old, and the King hath withdrawn all the honors he bestowed upon me, and not content with allowing me to wander and feed on grass, unprotected in my old age, he has *even caused me to be yoked to* the Potter's cart as are the oxen."

Then the Buddha promised that he would plead her cause, and appearing before the King, he asked: "Great King, did not a She-Elephant covered with weapons do battle for thee; and on such and such a day, with a writing upon her neck, did she not go a hundred leagues on a message? Thou didst bestow upon her great honor. I pray thee tell me, where is she now?"

And the King, in some confusion, made answer: "Behold, she is yoked to a cart."

Then did the Buddha speak in sorrowful anger to the King, and rebuked him, saying: "Thou hast yoked this Elephant to a cart after all the services she has rendered. Then was the honor only bestowed because of more services expected?"

And all who heard him received his instruction, and the King restored the She-Elephant to her former place of honor.

THE FAITHFUL FRIEND

THE FAITHFUL FRIEND

L ONG ago, when Brahma-datta was reigning in Benares, the Bodisat became his Minister.

At that time a dog used to go to the state elephant's stable, and feed on the lumps of rice which fell where the elephant fed. Being attracted there by the food, he soon became great friends with the elephant, and used to eat close by him. At last neither of them was happy without the other; and the dog used to amuse himself by catching hold of the elephant's trunk, and swinging to and fro.

But one day there came a peasant who gave the elephant-keeper money for the dog, and took it back with him to his village. From that time the elephant, missing the dog, would neither eat nor drink nor bathe. And they let the King know about it.

He sent the Bodisat, saying: "Do you·go,

Pandit, and find out what's the cause of the elephant's behavior."

So he went to the stable, and seeing how sad the elephant looked, said to himself: "There seems to be nothing bodily the matter with him. He must be so overwhelmed with grief by missing some one, I should think, who had become near and dear to him." And he asked the elephant-keepers: "Is there any one with whom he is particularly intimate?"

"Certainly, Sir! There was a dog of whom he was very fond indeed."

"Where is it now?"

"Some man or other took it away."

"Do you know where the man lives?"

"No, Sir!"

Then the Bodisat went and told the King. "There's nothing the matter with the elephant, your majesty; but he was great friends with a dog, and I fancy it's through missing it that he refuses his food."

When the King heard what he said, he asked what was now to be done.

"Have a proclamation made, O King, to this effect: 'A man is said to have taken away a dog of whom our state elephant was fond. In whose house soever that dog shall be found, he shall be fined so much!' "

The King did so; and, as soon as he heard of it, the man turned the dog loose. The dog hastened back, and went close up to the elephant. The elephant took him up in his trunk and placed him on his forehead, and wept and cried, and took him down again, and watched him as he fed. And then he took his own food.

Then the King paid great honor to the Bodisat for knowing the motives even of animals.

THE HAWK AND THE OSPREY

THE HAWK AND THE OSPREY

THERE lived once, on the shores of a natural lake, a Hawk on the south shore, a She-Hawk on the west shore, on the north a Lion, the king of beasts, on the east the Osprey, the king of birds, in the middle a Tortoise on a small island.

Now the Hawk asked the She-Hawk to become his wife. She asked him: "Have you any friends?" "No, madam," he replied. "But," she said, "we must have some friends who can defend us against any danger or trouble that may arise. Therefore I beg of you to find some friends." "But," said the Hawk, "with whom shall I make friends?" "Why, with King Osprey, who lives on the eastern shore, with King Lion on the north, and with the Tortoise who lives in the middle of the lake."

And he took her advice. And all these creatures formed a bond of friendship, and promised to protect each other in time of danger.

Now in time the Mother-Hawk had two sons. One day when the wings of the young birds were not yet callow, some of the country-folk went foraging through the woods all day and found nothing.

They went down to the lake to catch fish or a tortoise, and, in order to drive away the gnats, they made a fire by rubbing sticks together. The smoke annoyed the young birds, and they uttered a cry. The men said: " 'Tis the cry of birds—we will make a fire and eat their flesh." They made the fire blaze and built it up.

But the Mother-Bird heard the sound, and thought: "These men will eat our young ones. I will send my mate to the Great Osprey." This she did, and the bird promised to help. He sat upon a tree-top near that in which the Hawks had built their nests, and no sooner did the men begin to climb up the tree than the Osprey dived into the lake, and from wings and back sprinkled water upon the

brands and put the fire out. Down came the
men and made another fire, but again the
Osprey put it out, and this went on until
midnight.

And the bird was tired out and his eyes
were bloodshot. And the Mother - Bird
whispered to her mate: "My Lord, the Osprey
is worn out! Go and tell the Tortoise, that
this weary bird may have a rest."

But the Osprey in a loud voice said he
would gladly give his life to guard the tree.
And the grateful Hawk said: "I pray thee,
friend Osprey, rest awhile." Then he went
for help to the Tortoise, who said he would
gladly help, but his son said: "I would not
have my old father troubled, but I will gladly
go in his stead."

And the Tortoise collected mud and
quenched the flame. Then said the men: "Let
us kill the Tortoise: he will be enough for
all." But when they plucked creepers to bind
him and tried to turn him over, he dragged
them into the water. And they said: "What
strange things have happened to us! Half

the night the Osprey has put out our fire, and now the Tortoise has dragged us in after him and made us swallow water. Let us light another fire, and at sunrise we will eat these young Hawks."

The Hen-Bird heard the noise and said: "My husband—sooner or later these men will devour our young and depart. You go and tell our friend the Lion." At once the Hawk went to the Lion, who asked him why he came at such an unreasonable hour. But when the whole matter was put before him, he said: "Go and comfort your young ones, for I will save them." And then he came forth with a mighty tread, and the men were terrified.

"Alas!" they cried. "The Osprey hath put out our fire. The Tortoise dragged us into the water. But now we are done for: the Lion will destroy us at once." They ran this way and that, and when the noble beast stood at the foot of the tree, no trace could be found of the frightened men.

Then the Osprey, the Hawk, the She-Hawk, and the Tortoise came up to greet him, and they discoursed for a long time on the value of friendship. And this company of friends lived all their lives without breaking their bond. And they passed away according to their deeds.

GRANDMOTHER'S GOLDEN DISH

GRANDMOTHER'S GOLDEN DISH

LONG ago the Bodisat was a dealer in tin and brass ware, named Seriva, in the country of that name. This Seriva, together with another dealer in tin and brass ware, who was an avaricious man, crossed the river Tēlavāha, and entered the town called Andhapura. And, dividing the streets of the city between them, the Bodisat went round selling his goods in the street allotted to him, while the other took the street that fell to him.

Now in that city there was a wealthy family reduced to abject poverty. All the sons and brothers in the family had died, and all its property had been lost. Only one girl and her grandmother were left; and those two gained their living by serving others for hire. There was indeed in the house the vessel of gold out of which the head of the house used to eat in the days of its prosperity; but it was covered with dirt, and had long lain

neglected and unused among the pots and
pans. And they did not even know that it
was of gold.

At that time the avaricious hawker, as he
was going along, calling out, "Buy my water-
pots! Buy my water-pots!" came to the door
of their house. When the girl saw him, she
said to her grandmother: "Mother! do buy me
an ornament."

"But we are poor, dear. What shall we
give in exchange for it?"

"This dish of ours is no use to us; you can
give that away and get one."

The old woman called the hawker, and,
after asking him to take a seat, gave him
the dish, and said: "Will you take this, Sir,
and give something to your little sister for it?"

The hawker took the dish, and thought:
"This must be gold!" And turning it round,
he scratched a line on its back with a needle,
and found that it was so. Then, hoping to
get the dish without giving them anything,
he said: "What is this worth? It is not even
worth a halfpenny!" And throwing it on the

ground, he got up from his seat and went away.

Now, it was allowed to either hawker to enter the street which the other had left. And the Bodisat came into that street, and calling out, "Buy my water-pots," came up to the door of that very house. And the girl spoke to her grandmother as before. But the grandmother said: "My child, the dealer who came just now threw the dish on the floor, and went away; what have I now got to give him in exchange?"

"That merchant, mother dear, was a surly man; but this one looks pleasant, and has a kind voice: perchance he may take it."

"Call him, then," said she.

So she called him. And when he had come in and sat down, they gave him the dish. He saw that it was gold, and said: "Mother! this dish is worth a hundred thousand. All the goods in my possession are not equal to it in value!"

"But, Sir, a hawker who came just now threw it on the ground, and went away, saying it was not worth a halfpenny. It must have been changed into gold by the power of your virtue, so we make you a present of it."

The Bodisat gave them all the cash he had in hand (five hundred pieces), and all his stock-in-trade, worth five hundred more. He asked of them only to let him keep eight pennies, and the bag and the yoke that he used to carry his things with. And these he took and departed.

And going quickly to the river-side, he gave those eight pennies to a boatman, and got into the boat.

But the covetous hawker came back to the house, and said: "Bring out that dish, I'll give you something for it."

Then she scolded him, and said: "You said our gold dish, worth a hundred thousand, was not worth a halfpenny. But a just dealer, who seems to be your master, gave us a thousand for it, and has taken it away."

When he heard this he called out: "Through this fellow I have lost a golden pot worth—Oh, worth a hundred thousand! He has ruined me altogether!" And bitter sorrow overcame him, and he was unable to retain his presence of mind, and he lost all self-command. And scattering the money he had, and all the goods, at the door of the house, he seized as a club the yoke by which he had carried them, and tore off his clothes, and pursued after the Bodisat.

When he reached the river-side, he saw the Bodisat going away, and he cried out: "Hallo, Boatman! stop the boat!"

But the Bodisat said: "Don't stop!" and so prevented that. And as the other gazed and gazed at the departing Bodisat, he was torn with violent grief; his heart grew hot, and blood flowed from his mouth until his heart broke—like tank-mud in the heat of the sun.

Thus harboring hatred against the Bodisat, he brought about on that very spot his own destruction. This was the first time that Devadatta harbored hatred against the Bodisat.

But the Bodisat gave gifts, and did other good acts, and passed away according to his deeds.

THE ELEPHANT THAT SPARED LIFE

THE ELEPHANT THAT SPARED LIFE

A T that time the Bodisat was born as a
nobleman's son. On the naming-day
they gave him the name of Prince Magha, and
when he grew up he was known as "Magha
the young Brahmin."

His parents procured him a wife from a
family of equal rank; and, increasing in sons
and daughters, he became a great giver of
gifts, and kept the Five Commandments.

In that village there were as many as thirty
families; and one day the men of those
families stopped in the middle of the village
to transact some village business. The Bodisat
removed with his feet the lumps of soil on
the place where he stood, and made the spot
convenient to stand on; but another came up
and stood there. Then he smoothed out another spot, and took his stand there; but another man came and stood upon it. Still the

Bodisat tried again and again, with the same result, until he had made convenient standing-room for all the thirty.

The next time he had an open-roofed shed put up there; and then pulled that down, and built a hall, and had benches spread in it, and a water-pot placed there. On another occasion those thirty men were reconciled by the Bodisat, who confirmed them in the Five Commandments; and thenceforward he continued with them in works of piety.

Whilst they were so living they used to rise up early, go out with bill-hooks and crow-bars in their hands, tear up with the crowbars the stones in the four high roads and village paths, and roll them away, take away the trees which would be in the way of vehicles, make the rough places plain, form causeways, dig ponds, build public halls, give gifts, and keep the Commandments—thus, in many ways, all the dwellers in the village listened to the exhortations of the Bodisat, and kept the Commandments.

Now the village headman said to himself:

"I used to have great gain from fines, and taxes, and pot-money, when these fellows drank strong drink, or took life, or broke the other Commandments. But now Magha the young Brahmin has determined to have the Commandments kept, and permits none to take life, or to do anything else that is wrong. I'll make them keep the Commandments with a vengeance!"

And he went in a rage to the King, and said: "O King! there are a number of robbers going about sacking the villages!"

"Go and bring them up!" said the King in reply.

And he went, and brought back all those men as prisoners, and had it announced to the King that the robbers were brought up. And the King, without inquiring what they had done, gave orders to have them all trampled to death by elephants!

Then they made them all lie down in the courtyard, and fetched the elephant. And the Bodisat exhorted them, saying: "Keep the Commandments in mind. Regard them all—

the slanderer, and the King, and the elephant
—with feelings as kind as you harbor towards yourselves!"

And they did so.

Then men led up the elephant; but though
they brought him to the spot, he would not
begin his work, but trumpeted forth a mighty
cry, and took to flight. And they brought up
another and another, but they all ran away.

"There must be some drug in their possession," said the King; and gave orders to have
them searched. So they searched, but found
nothing, and told the King so.

"Then they must be repeating some spell.
Ask them if they have any spell to utter."

The officials asked them, and the Bodisat
said there was. And they told the King, and
he had them all called before him, and said:
"Tell me that spell you know!"

Then the Bodisat spoke, and said: "O King!
we have no other spell but this—that we destroy no life, not even of grass; that we take
nothing which is not given to us; that we are
never guilty of unfaithfulness, nor speak
falsehood, nor drink intoxicants; that we ex-

ercise ourselves in love, and give gifts; that we make rough places plain, dig ponds, and put up rest-houses—this is our spell, this is our defense, this is our strength!"

Then the King had confidence in them, and gave them all the property in the house of the slanderer, and made him their slave; and bestowed, too, the elephant upon them, and made them a grant of the village.

HOW THE ANTELOPE WAS
CAUGHT

HOW THE ANTELOPE WAS CAUGHT

ONCE upon a time the King of Benares had a gardener named Sanjaya. Now, a swift antelope who had come to the garden took to flight as soon as it saw Sanjaya. But Sanjaya did not frighten it away; and when it had come again and again it began to walk about in the garden. And day by day the gardener used to pluck the various fruits and flowers in the garden and take them away to the King.

Now, one day the King asked him: "I say, friend gardener, is there anything strange in the garden so far as you've noticed?"

"I've noticed nothing, O King, save that an antelope is in the habit of coming and wandering about there. That I often see."

"But could you catch it?"

"If I had a little honey I could bring it right inside the palace here!"

The King gave him the honey; and he took it, went to the garden, smeared it on the grass at the spot the antelope frequented, and hid himself. When the deer came and had eaten the honey-smeared grass, it was bound with the lust of taste; and from that time went nowhere else, but came exclusively to the garden. And as the gardener saw that it was allured by the honey-smeared grass, he in due course showed himself. For a few days the antelope took to flight on seeing him. But after seeing him again and again it acquired confidence, and gradually came to eat grass from the gardener's hand. And when the gardener saw that its confidence was gained, he strewed the path right up to the palace as thick with branches as if he were covering it with mats, hung a gourdful of honey over his shoulder, carried a bundle of grass at his waist, and then kept sprinkling honey-smeared grass in front of the antelope till he led him within the palace.

As soon as the deer had got inside, they shut the door. The antelope, seeing men, began to tremble and quake with the fear of death, and ran hither and thither about the hall. The King came down from his upper chamber, and, seeing the trembling creature, said: "Such is the nature of an antelope, that it will not go for a week afterwards to a place where it has seen men, nor its life long to a place where it has been frightened. Yet this one, with just such a disposition, and accustomed only to the jungle, has now, bound by the lust of taste, come to just such a place. Verily, there is nothing worse in the world than this lust of taste!"

And when in other words he had shown the danger of greed, he let the antelope go back to the forest.

THE BANYAN DEER

THE BANYAN DEER

LONG ago the Bodisat came to life as a
deer. When he was born he was of a
golden color; his eyes were like round jewels;
his horns were white as silver; his mouth was
red as a cluster of kamala flowers; his hoofs
were as bright and hard as lacquer-work; his
tail as fine as the tail of a Thibetan ox; and
his body as large in size as a foal's.

He lived in the forest with an attendant
herd of five hundred deer, under the name of
the King of the Banyan Deer; and not far
from him there dwelt another deer, golden as
he, under the name of the Monkey Deer, with
a like attendant herd.

The King of that country was devoted to
hunting, never ate without meat, and used to
summon all the townspeople to go hunting
every day to the destruction of their ordinary
work. The people thought, "This King puts
an end to all our work. Suppose we make a

park, provide food and drink for the deer.
Then we will drive them into the park, close
the entrance and deliver them to the King."

This they did, surrounding the very place
where the Banyan Deer and the Monkey Deer
were living. When the King heard this, he
went to the park, and seeing there the two
golden-colored deer, he granted them their
lives. But henceforth he would go himself to
shoot the deer and bring it home. Sometimes
his cook would go and shoot one. The deer,
as soon as they saw the bow, would quake with
fear of Death, and run away; but when they
had been hit once or twice, they became weary
or wounded and were killed. And the herd
told their King, who sent for the Monkey
Deer and said: "Friend, almost all the Deer
are being destroyed. Now, though they certainly must die, yet henceforth let them not
be wounded with arrows. Let the deer take
it by turns to go to the place of execution.
One day let the lot fall on my herd, and the
next day on yours."

He agreed, and thenceforth the deer whose
turn it was used to go down and lie down after

placing his neck on the block of execution. And the cook used to come and carry off the one he found lying there.

But one day the lot fell upon a roe in the Monkey Deer who was with young. She went to the Monkey Deer and said: "Lord! I am with young. When I have brought forth my son, we will both take our turn. Order the bows to pass me by."

"I cannot make your lot," said he, "fall upon the others. You know well enough it has fallen upon you. Go away!" Receiving no help from him, she went to the Bodisat and told him the matter. He listened to her quietly and said: "Be it so! Do you go back. I will relieve you of your turn." And he went himself and laid his head on the block of execution.

The cook, seeing him, exclaimed: "The King of the Deer whose life was promised to him is lying in the place of execution. What does it mean?" And he went hastily, and told the King.

The King no sooner heard it than he mounted his chariot and proceeded with a great retinue to the place, and beholding the Bodisat, said: "My friend, the King of the Deer! Did I not grant you your life? Why are you lying here?"

"O great King! A roe with young came and told me that the lot had fallen upon her. Now I could not ask another to take her place, so I, giving my life for her, have lain down. Harbor no further suspicion, O great King!"

"My Lord, the golden-colored King of the Deer! I never yet saw, even among men, one so full of forbearance, kindness and compassion. I am pleased with thee in this matter! Rise up. I grant your lives, both to you and to her!"

"But though we be safe, what shall the rest do, O King of men?"

"Then I grant their lives to the rest, my Lord."

"Thus, then, great King, the deer in the park will have gained security, but what will the others do?"

"They also shall not be molested."

"Great King! even though the deer dwell

secure, what shall the rest of the four-footed creatures do?"

"They shall also be free from fear."

"Great King, even though the quadrupeds are in safety, what shall the flock of birds do?"

"Well, I grant the same boon to them."

"Great King! the birds then will obtain peace; but what of the fish who dwell in the water?"

"They shall have peace as well."

Then the Great Being having interceded with the King for all creatures, said:

"Walk in righteousness, O great King! Doing justice to fathers and mothers, to townsmen and landsmen, you shall enter, when your body is dissolved, the happy world of Heaven."

*   *   *   *   *

The roe gave birth to a son as beautiful as buds of flowers; and he went to playing about with the Monkey Deer's herd. But when its mother saw that, she said, "My son, henceforth go not in his company. You may keep to the Banyan Deer's herd."

Now after that, the deer, secure of their lives, began to eat men's crops. And the men dared not strike them or drive them away, recollecting how it had been granted to them that they should dwell secure. So they met together in front of the King's palace, and told the matter to the King.

"When I was well pleased, I granted to the leader of the Banyan herd a boon," said he. "I may give up my kingdom but not my oaths! Begone with you! Not a man in my kingdom shall be allowed to hurt the deer."

When the Banyan King heard that, he assembled his herd, and said:

"Henceforth you are not allowed to eat other people's crops." And so forbidding them, he sent a message to the men: "Henceforth let the husbandmen put up no fence to guard their crops: but let them tie leaves round the edge of the field as a sign."

From that time, they say, the sign of the tying of the leaves was seen in the fields, and from that time not a single deer trespassed beyond it: for such was the instruction they

received from (their King) the Bodisat.
And the Bodisat continued thus his life long
to instruct the deer, and passed away with
his herd, according to his deeds.

THE PUPIL WHO TAUGHT HIS TEACHER

(From *"Buddhist Birth Stories."*)

THE PUPIL WHO TAUGHT HIS TEACHER

AND the Buddha was re-born in a Brahmin family and was known as Dhamapala or Law Keeper.

When he came of age he was sent by his father to study with a world famed teacher at Takasila and became the chief pupil in a company of five hundred youths.

At that time the eldest son of the teacher died and the father, surrounded by his pupils, in the midst of his kith and kin, buried his son —and all the pupils wept and wailed, but Dhamapala was silent and shed no tear, but when the company returned from the cemetery Dhamapala asked, "Why did your son die? It is not right that children should die; only when people grow old can this happen." And they asked him, "Is it the custom of your family that the young do not die?" And he said: "Yes, that is the custom in my family."

The lads told this conversation to their teacher.

Now when the teacher heard this, he said to them, "That is a most marvelous thing that he says. I will make a journey to his father and ask him about it, and if it be true I will live according to his rule of right."

And he said to the young man: "I am going on a journey. Do thou, in my absence, instruct these youths."

So saying, he procured the bones of a wild goat, washed and scented them, and put them into a bag. Then taking with him a little page boy he started for the village in which lived the father of his pupil.

When the house was reached, and the teacher had rested and taken food, and the host had washed the feet of his guest, the teacher said: " Brahmin, your son when full of wisdom has by an unhappy chance lost his life. Grieve not for him." The Brahmin laughed loudly. "Why do you laugh, Brahmin?" asked the other. "Because," he said, "it is *not* my son who is dead; it must be some other."

"No, Brahmin, your son is dead, and no

other. Look on his bones, and believe." So saying, he unwrapped the bones. "There are your son's bones," he said.

"A wild goat's bones, perhaps," quoth the Brahmin, "or a dog's, but my son is not dead. In our family for seven generations, no such thing has been known as a death in tender years, and you are speaking falsehood." Then they all clapped their hands and laughed aloud.

The teacher, when he beheld this wonderful thing, was much pleased and said: "Brahmin, this custom in your family line cannot be without cause, that the young do not die. Why *is* it that you do not die young? Of what good and holy deed is this the fruit?"

Then the Brahmin made answer:

"We walk in righteousness. We speak no ill. We flee from things that are evil. We take no heed of the foolish. We follow the counsel of the wise. We delight in giving gifts. We feed the hungry. We are faithful in our marriage vows. We are versed in sacred knowledge. Therefore, the young amongst us never die."

On hearing this, the teacher replied: "A

happy journey is this of mine and fruitful. I came hither, O wise Brahmin, to test you. Your son is safe and well. I pray you impart to me your rule of preserving life."

Then the other wrote it on a leaf and returned to his pupils.

THE MAN WHO TOLD A LIE

THE MAN WHO TOLD A LIE

ON one occasion four divine beings made their appearance on the Earth to attend a festival of the Gods.

And they bore in their hands wreaths of the strangest flowers that had ever been seen, and those around asked: "What are these flowers?" And the Gods made answer and said: "These divine flowers are fit for those possessed of great powers: for the base, the foolish, the faithless, the sinful beings within the world of men, they are *not* fitted. But, whosoever amongst men is endowed with certain virtues—to them is due the honor of wearing these flowers.

> "He who steals no thing from another,
> Who uttereth no lie,
> Who doth not lose his head at the
>   height of Fame—
> He may wear the flowers."

147

Now there was a certain false Teacher or Priest who thought to himself: "I do not possess one of these qualities, but, by appearing to possess them, I shall obtain permission to wear the wreaths, and the people will believe that I really am what I appear to be, and they will place their confidence in me."

Then, with exceeding boldness, he came to the first of the Gods and exclaimed with great solemnity: "Behold, *I* am endowed with these qualities of which you speak—

"I have stolen from no man, never have I uttered a lie, nor has fame ever caused me to be proud or haughty."

And when he had uttered these words, the wreath was placed upon his brow. And, emboldened by his success, he came with the same pride and confidence into the presence of the second God, and asked that the second wreath should be bestowed upon him.

And the God said:

"He who earns wealth honestly, and shuns dishonest means,

Who takes but sparingly of the Cup of
    Pleasure,
To him shall be awarded this second
    wreath."

And the false Priest bowed his head and
said: "Behold all that I have earned is
honestly gotten, and all pleasure have I
shunned. Give me the wreath!"

And the wreath was placed upon his
brow.

Then, with boldness increased by his
success, he approached the third God, and
asked that the third wreath should encircle
his brow.

And the God said:

"He who scorns choice food,
Who never turneth from his purpose,
Who keepeth his faith unchanged,
To him shall be given the wreath."

And the false Priest said: "I have ever lived
on the simplest fare. I have been ever stead-

fast of purpose, and loyal in my faith. Therefore give *me* the wreath."

And the third wreath was bestowed upon him.

Then did the pride of the false Priest know no bounds, and he went hastily to the fourth God and demanded the fourth wreath.

And the God said:

"He who will attack no good man to his
face or behind his back,
And who keeps his word in all things,
To him belongs this wreath."

Then the false Priest cried out in a loud voice: "I have attacked no man, good or evil, and never have I broken my word to any."

The God looked at him sadly, but he placed the wreath upon his brow, and the four divine beings disappeared from the sight of man. But no sooner had they left the earth than the Priest felt a violent pain. His head seemed to be crushed by spikes, and, writhing in agony, he made full confession and begged that the flowers should be removed from his head; but though all pitied his condition, none could remove the flowers, for they seemed to be fastened on with an iron band.

And he called aloud to the Gods, saying

"O ye great powers, forgive my pride and spare my life!" And they answered: "These flowers are not meet for the wicked. You have received the reward of your false words." Then, having rebuked him in the presence of the people, they removed the flowers from the head of the repentant man and returned to the abode of the Blest.

THE CROW THAT THOUGHT IT KNEW

THE CROW THAT THOUGHT IT KNEW

ONCE upon a time, while Brahma-datta reigned as king in Benares, the Bodhisatta became a marsh crow, and dwelt by a certain pool. His name was Viraka, the Strong.

There arose a famine in Kasi. Men could not spare food for the crows, nor make offering to goblins and snakes. One by one the crows left the famine-stricken land, and betook them to the woods.

A certain crow named Savitthaka, who lived at Benares, took with him his lady crow and went to the place where Viraka lived, making his abode beside the same pool.

One day, this crow was seeking food about the pool. He saw how Viraka went down into it, and made a meal off some fish; and afterwards came up out of the water again, and stood drying his feathers. "Under the wing of that crow," thought he, "plenty of fish are to be got. I will become his servant." So he drew near.

"What is it, Sir?" asked Viraka.

"I want to be your servant, my Lord!" was the reply.

Viraka agreed, and from that time the other served him. And from that time, Viraka used to eat enough fish to keep him alive, and the rest he gave to Savitthaka as soon as he had caught them; and when Savitthaka had eaten enough to keep him alive, he gave what was over to his wife.

After a while pride came into his heart. "This crow," said he, "is black, and so am I: in eyes and beak and feet, too, there is no difference between us. I don't want his fish; I will catch my own!" So he told Viraka that for the future he intended to go down to the water and catch fish himself. Then Viraka said, "Good friend, you do not belong to a tribe of such crows as are born to go into water and catch fish. Don't destroy yourself!"

But in spite of this attempt to dissuade him, Savitthaka did not take the warning to heart.

Down he went to the pool, into the water; but he could not make his way through the weeds and come out again—there he was, entangled in the weeds, with only the tip of his beak appearing above the water. So not being able to breathe he perished there beneath the water.

His mate noticed that he did not return, and went to Viraka to ask news of him. "My Lord," she asked, "Savitthaka is not to be seen: where is he?" And as she asked him this, she repeated the first stanza:—

"O have you seen Savitthaka, O Viraka,
    have you seen
My sweet-voiced mate whose neck is like
    the peacock in its sheen?"

When Viraka heard it, he replied, "Yes, I know where he is gone," and recited the second stanza:—

"He was not born to dive beneath
    the wave,
    But what he could not do he
    needs must try;

So the poor bird has found a watery
    grave,
    Entangled in the weeds, and left
      to die."

When the lady-crow heard it, weeping, she
returned to Benares.

THE JUDAS TREE

THE JUDAS TREE

ONCE upon a time Brahmadatta, the king of Benares, had four sons. One day they sent for the charioteer, and said to him:

"We want to see a Judas tree; show us one!"

"Very well, I will," the charioteer replied. But he did not show it to them all together. He took the eldest at once to the forest in the chariot, and showed him the tree at the time when the buds were just sprouting from the stem. To the second he showed it when the leaves were green, to the third at the time of blossoming, and to the fourth when it was bearing fruit.

After this it happened that the four brothers were sitting together, and some one asked, "What sort of a tree is the Judas tree?" Then the first brother answered:

"Like a burnt stump!"

And the second cried, "Like a banyan tree!"

And the third—"Like a piece of meat!"

And the fourth said, "Like the acacia!"

They were vexed at each other's answers, and ran to find their father. "My Lord," they asked, "what sort of a tree is the Judas tree?"

"What did you say to that?" he asked. They told him the manner of their answers. Said the king:

"All four of you have seen the tree. Only when the charioteer showed you the tree, you did not ask him, 'What is the tree like at such a time?' or 'at such another time?' You made no distinctions, and that is the reason for your mistake." And he repeated the first stanza:—

"All have seen the Judas tree—
What is your perplexity?
No one asked the charioteer
What its form the livelong year!"

THE RIVER FISH AND THE MONEY

THE RIVER FISH AND THE MONEY

ONCE upon a time, when Brahmadatta was king of Benares, the Bodhisatta was born in the family of a landed proprietor. When he grew up, he became a wealthy man. He had a young brother. Afterwards their father died. They determined to arrange some business of their father's. This took them to a village, where they were paid a thousand pieces of money. On their way back, as they waited on a river-bank for the boat, they ate a meal out of a leaf-pottle. The Bodhisatta threw what he left into the Ganges for the fishes, giving the merit to the river-spirit. The spirit accepted this with gratification, which increased her divine power, and on thinking over this increase of her power, became aware what had happened. The Bodhisatta laid his upper garment upon the sand, and there he lay down and went to sleep.

Now the young brother was of a rather thievish nature. He wanted to filch the money from the Bodhisatta and keep it himself; so he packed a parcel of gravel to look like the parcel of money, and put them both away.

When they had got aboard, and were come to mid-river, the younger stumbled against the side of the boat, and dropped overboard the parcel of gravel, as he thought, but really the money.

"Brother, the money's overboard!" he cried. "What's to be done?"

"What can we do? What's gone is gone. Never mind about it," replied the other.

But the river-spirit thought how pleased she had been with the merit she had received, and how her divine power had been increased, and resolved to take care of his property. So by her power she made a big-mouthed fish swallow the parcel, and took care of it herself.

When the thief got home, he chuckled over the trick he had served his brother, and undid

the remaining parcel. There was nothing but
gravel to be seen! His heart dried up; he fell
on his bed, and clutched the bedstead.

Now some fishermen just then cast their
nets for a draught. By power of the river-
spirit, this fish fell into the net. The fishers
took it to town to sell. People asked what the
price was.

"A thousand pieces and seven annas," said
the fishermen.

Everybody made fun of them. "We have
seen a fish offered for a thousand pieces!" they
laughed.

The fishers brought their fish to the Bodhisatta's door, and asked him to buy it.

"What's the price?" he asked.

"You may have it for seven annas," they
said.

"What did you ask other people for it?"

"From other people we asked a thousand
rupees and seven annas; but you may have it
for seven annas," they said.

He paid seven annas for it, and sent it to
his wife. She cut it open, and there was the

parcel of money! She called the Bodhisatta. He gave a look, and recognizing his mark, knew it for his own. Thought he, "These fishers asked other people the price of a thousand rupees and seven annas, but because the thousand rupees were mine, they let me have it for seven annas only! If a man does not understand the meaning of this, nothing will ever make him believe."

When he had said this, he wondered how it was that he had recovered his money. At the moment the river-spirit hovered invisibly in the air, and declared—

"I am the Spirit of the Ganges. You gave the remains of your meal to the fishes, and let me have the merit. Therefore I have taken care of your property."

Then the Spirit told about the mean trick which the younger brother had played. Then she added, "There he lies, with his heart dried up within him. There is no prosperity for the cheat. But I have brought you your own, and I warn you not to lose it. Don't give it to your young thief of a brother, but keep it all yourself."

Thus spoke the Spirit, not wishing that the treacherous villain should receive the money. But the Bodhisatta said, "That is impossible," and all the same sent the brother five hundred.

THE DREAMER IN THE WOOD

THE DREAMER IN THE WOOD

NOW the Buddha once upon a time lived alone in the woods, in the ecstasy of meditation. For wild fruits he went no further afield. When fruit grew upon the tree, he ate the fruit; in time of flowers, he ate flowers. When the leaves grew, he ate leaves. When leaves were none, he ate the bark of trees. Thus, in the highest contentment he lived a long time in that place.

Now on a day, Sakka, the King of the gods, appeared before him and, wishing to test him, said: "Behold yon man, all black of hue, my spirit likes him not."

Now by his divine insight the Buddha knew that Sakka spoke to him. And he made answer and said:

"Though black of hue, I am a true Brahmin. A man is not black by reason of his outer skin; only can sin make him black." Thus he discoursed to Sakka, and it was as he had made the moon to rise in the sky. And the god asked him what boon he would crave.

And the Divine being asked to be free of three things: malice, hatred and greed.

Then Sakka: "What is bad in these things?" And Buddha made answer, "Because hatred grows from small to great and is ever full of bitterness. Malice brings evil. First word, then touch, next fist, then staff, and last the swordstroke flashing free. When men are urged by greed, then arise fraud and deceit and swift pursuit of savage loot——"

"Then," said Sakka, "choose another boon."

Then said the Buddha, "Grant that in the woods where I live alone, no disease may mar my peace, or break my ecstasy."

Then said Sakka, "He chooseth no thing connected with food." And he granted yet another boon.

And the Buddha said, "Let no creature ever be harmed for me in body or in mind."

And Sakka made the tree bear fruit perennially, and saluting the Buddha by touching his head with joined hands, he said:

"Dwell here for ever free from disease," and returned to his throne.

THE RICE MEASURE

THE RICE MEASURE

LONG ago, Brahmadatta was king in Benares, in the land of Kāsi. At that time our Bodisat was his valuer. He valued both horses, elephants, or things of that kind; and jewelry, gold, or things of that kind; and having done so, he used to have the proper price for the goods given to the owners thereof.

Now the King was covetous. And in his avarice he thought, "If this valuer estimates in this way, it will not be long before all the wealth in my house will come to an end. I will appoint another valuer."

And opening his window, and looking out into the palace yard, he saw a stupid miserly peasant crossing the yard. Him he determined to make his valuer; and sending for him, asked if he would undertake the office. The man said he could; and the King, with the object of keeping his treasure safer, established that fool in the post of valuer.

Thenceforward the dullard used to value the horses and elephants, paying no regard to their real value, but deciding just as he chose; and since he had been appointed to the office, as he decided, so the price was.

Now at that time a horse-dealer brought five hundred horses from the northern prairies. The King sent for that fellow, and had the horses valued. And he valued the five hundred horses at a mere measure of rice, and straightway ordered the horse-dealer to be given the measure of rice, and the horses to be lodged in the stable. Then the horse-dealer went to the former valuer, and told him what had happened, and asked him what he should do.

"Give a bribe to that fellow," said he, "and ask him thus: 'We know now that so many horses of ours are worth a measure of rice, but we want to know from you what a measure of rice is worth. Can you value it for us, standing in your place by the King?' If he says he can, go with him into the royal presence, and I will be there too."

The horse-dealer accepted the Bodisat's

advice, went to the valuer, and bribed him,
and gave him the hint suggested. And he
took the bribe, and said, "All right! I can
value your measure of rice for you."

"Well, then, let us go to the audience-hall,"
said he; and taking him with him, went into
the King's presence. And the Bodisat and
many other ministers went there also.

The horse-dealer bowed down before the
King, and said, "I acknowledge, O King, that
a measure of rice is the value of the five
hundred horses; but will the King be pleased
to ask the valuer what the value of the measure
of rice may be?"

The King, not knowing what had happened,
asked, "How now, valuer, *what* are five hundred horses worth?"

"A measure of rice, O King!" said he.

"Very good, then! If five hundred horses
are worth only a measure of rice, what is that
measure of rice worth?"

"The measure of rice is worth all Benares,
both within and without the walls," replied
that foolish fellow.

For the story goes that he first valued the

horses at a measure of rice just to please the King; and then, when he had taken the dealer's bribe, valued that measure of rice at the whole of Benares. Now at that time the circumference of the rampart of Benares was twelve leagues, and the land in its suburbs was three hundred leagues in extent. Yet the foolish fellow estimated that so-great city of Benares, together with all its suburbs, at a measure of rice!

Hearing this the ministers clapped their hands, laughing, and saying, "We used to think the broad earth, and the King's realm, were alike beyond price; but this great and famous royal city is worth, by his account, just a measure of rice! O the depth of the wisdom of the valuer! How can he have stayed so long in office? Truly he is just suited to our King!" Thus they laughed him to scorn.

Then the Bodisat uttered this stanza:

"What is a measure of rice worth?
All Benares and its environs!

And what are five hundred horses
    worth?
That same measure of rice!"

Then the king was ashamed, and drove out
ıat fool, and appointed the Bodisat to the
ffice of valuer. And in course of time the
ıodisat passed away according to his deeds.

THE POISONOUS TREES

THE POISONOUS TREES

ONCE upon a time when Brahmadatta was reigning in Benares, the Bodhisatta was born a merchant. When he grew up, and was trading with five hundred wagons, he came one day to where the road led through a great forest. Halting at the outskirts, he mustered the caravan and addressed them thus:— "Poison-trees grow in this forest. Take heed that you taste no unfamiliar leaf, flower, or fruit without first consulting me." All promised to take every care; and the journey into the forest began. Now just within the forest-border stands a village, and just outside that village grows a What-fruit tree. That What-fruit tree exactly resembles a mango alike in trunk, branch, leaf, flower, and fruit. And not only in outward semblance, but also in taste and smell, the fruit—ripe and unripe—mimics the mango. If eaten, it is a deadly poison, and causes instant death.

Now some greedy fellows, who went on ahead of the caravan, came to this tree and, taking it to be a mango, ate of its fruit. But others said, "Let us ask our leader before we eat"; and they accordingly halted by the tree, fruit in hand, till he came up. Perceiving that it was no mango, he said:—"This 'mango' is a What-fruit tree; don't touch its fruit."

Having stopped them from eating, the Bodhisatta turned his attention to those who had already eaten. First he dosed them with an emetic, and then he gave them the four sweet foods to eat; so that in the end they recovered.

Now on former occasions caravans had halted beneath this same tree, and had died from eating the poisonous fruit which they mistook for mangoes. On the morrow the villagers would come, and seeing them lying there dead, would fling them by the heels into a secret place, departing with all the belongings of the caravan, wagons and all.

And on the day too of our story these villagers failed not to hurry at daybreak to the tree for their expected spoils. "The oxen

must be ours," said some. "And we'll have
the wagons," said others;—whilst others
again claimed the wares as their share. But
when they came breathless to the tree, there
was the whole caravan alive and well!

"How came you to know this was not a
mango tree?" demanded the disappointed villagers. "We didn't know," said they of the
caravan; "it was our leader who knew."

So the villagers came to the Bodhisatta and
said, "Man of wisdom, what did you do to
find out this tree was not a mango?"

"Two things told me," replied the Bodhisatta, and he repeated this stanza:—

"When near a village grows a tree
Not hard to climb, 'tis plain to me,
Nor need I further proof to know,
—No wholesome fruit thereon can grow!"

And having taught the Truth to the assembled multitude, he finished his journey in
safety.

THE WELL-TRAINED ELEPHANT

THE WELL-TRAINED ELEPHANT

ONCE upon a time when King Magadha was ruling in Rajagaha in Magadha, the Bodhisatta was born an elephant. He was white all over and graced with all beauty. And because of his beauty the King made him his state elephant.

One festal day the King adorned the city like a city of the devas and, mounted on the elephant in all its trappings, made a solemn procession round the city attended by a great retinue. And all along the route the people were moved by the sight of that peerless elephant to exclaim, "Oh, what a stately gait! what proportions! what beauty! what grace! such a white elephant is worthy of an universal monarch." All this praise of his elephant awoke the King's jealousy and he resolved to have it cast over a precipice and killed. So he summoned the mahout and asked whether he called that a trained elephant.

"Indeed he is well trained, Sire," said the mahout. "No, he is very badly trained." "Sire, he is well trained." "If he is so well trained, can you get him to climb to the summit of Mount Vepulla?" "Yes, Sire." "Away with you, then," said the King. And he got down from the elephant, making the mahout mount instead, and went himself to the foot of the mountain, whilst the mahout rode on the elephant's back up to the top of Mount Vepulla. The King with his courtiers also climbed the mountain, and had the elephant halted at the brink of a precipice. "Now," said he to the man, "if he is so well trained as you say, make him stand on three legs."

And the mahout on the elephant's back just touched the animal with his goad by way of sign and called to him, "Hi! my beauty, stand on three legs." "Now make him stand on his two fore-legs," said the King. And the Great Being raised his hind-legs and stood on his fore-legs alone. "Now on the hind-legs," said the King, and the obedient elephant raised his fore-legs till he stood on his hind-legs alone.

"Now on one leg," said the King, and the elephant stood on one leg.

Seeing that the elephant did not fall over the precipice, the King cried, "Now if you can, make him stand in the air."

Then thought the mahout to himself, "All India cannot show the match of this elephant for excellence of training. Surely the King must want to make him tumble over the precipice and meet his death." So he whispered in the elephant's ear, "My son, the King wants you to fall over and get killed. He is not worthy of you. If you have power to journey through the air, rise up with me upon your back and fly through the air to Benares."

And the Great Being, endowed as he was with the marvelous powers which flow from Merit, straightway rose up into the air. Then said the mahout, "Sire, this elephant, possessed as he is with the marvelous powers which flow from Merit, is too good for such a worthless fool as you: none but a wise and good King is worthy to be his master. When those who are so worthless as you get an ele-

phant like this, they don't know his value, and
so they lose their elephant, and all the rest of
their glory and splendor." So saying the
mahout, seated on the elephant's neck, recited
this stanza:—

"Exalted station breeds a fool great woe;
He proves his own and others' mortal foe."

"And now, good-by," said he to the King
as he ended this rebuke; and rising in the air,
he passed to Benares and halted in mid-air,
over the royal courtyard. And there was a
great stir in the city and all cried out, "Look
at the state-elephant that has come through
the air for our King and is hovering over the
royal courtyard." And with all haste the news
was conveyed to the King, too, who came out
and said, "If your coming is for my behoof,
alight on the earth." And the Bodhisatta
descended from the air. Then the mahout got
down and bowed before the King, and in answer to the King's enquiries told the whole
story of their leaving Rajagaha. "It was very
good of you," said the King, "to come here";

and in his joy he had the city decorated and the elephant installed in his state-stable. Then he divided his kingdom into three portions, and made over one to the Bodhisatta, one to the mahout, and one he kept himself. And his power grew from the day of the Bodisatta's coming till all India owned his sovereign sway. As Emperor of India, he was charitable and did other good works till he passed away to fare according to his deserts.

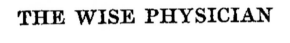

THE WISE PHYSICIAN

THE WISE PHYSICIAN

KISĀGOTAMI is the name of a young
girl, whose marriage with the only son
of a wealthy man was brought about in true
fairy-tale fashion. She had one child, but
when the beautiful boy could run alone, it died.
The young girl in her love for it carried
the dead child clasped to her bosom, and went
from house to house of her pitying friends
asking them to give her medicine for it. But
a Buddhist mendicant, thinking, "She does
not understand," said to her: "My good girl,
I myself have no such medicine as you ask
for, but I think I know of one who has." "Oh,
tell me who that is!" said Kisāgotamī. "The
Buddha can give you medicine: go to him,"
was the answer.

She went to Gautama, and doing homage
to him, said: "Lord and Master, do you know
any medicine that will be good for my child?"
"Yes, I know of some," said the Teacher.

Now it was the custom for patients or their friends to provide the herbs which the doctors required, so she asked what herbs he would want. "I want some mustard-seed," he said; and when the poor girl eagerly promised to bring some of so common a drug, he added: "You must get it from some house where no son, or husband, or parent, or slave has died." "Very good," she said, and went to ask for it, still carrying her dead child with her. The people said: "Here is mustard-seed, take it." But when she asked, "In my friend's house has any son died, or a husband, or a parent, or slave?" they answered: "Lady! what is this that thou sayest; the living are few, but the dead are many." Then she went to other houses, but one said: "I have lost a son"; another, "We have lost our parents"; another, "I have lost my slave."

At last, not being able to find a single house where no one had died, her mind began to clear, and, summoning up resolution, she left the dead body of her child in a forest, and returning to the Buddha paid him homage. He said to her: "Have you the mustard-

seed?" "My Lord," she replied, " I have not;
the people tell me that the living are few, but
the dead are many." Then he talked to her
on that essential part of his system—the
impermanency of all things, till her doubts
were cleared away, and, accepting her lot, she
became a disciple and entered the first Path.

The following lines, ascribed to some of her Sisters
in the Order and given in the *Psalms* (translated by
Mrs. Rhys Davids), would apply to Kisāgotamī:—
"Lo! from my heart the hidden shaft is gone,
  The shaft that nestled there hath he removed;
And that consuming grief for my dear child,
  Which poisoned all the life of me, is dead.
To-day my heart is healed, my yearning stayed,
  Perfected the deliverance wrought in me."

NOTES FOR TEACHERS

THE following notes are intended for teachers who may wish to use this collection as a class text book. In all these stories we have the idea of the Indian God in various re-incarnations until he has attained full Buddhahood. Beyond occasionally mentioning the fact of Re-birth in introducing the story (so as to preserve the Oriental flavor) I do not insist on this, nor do I introduce the name of the Buddha into the actual table of contents at the beginning of the book, as it might seem abstruse to the younger readers. But because I wish to appeal to scholars in the higher sense as well as to boys and girls, I have tried in many instances to preserve the language as given in the translation from the Pali. I have also tried to avoid cutting out any important episodes; this sometimes happens in the popular adaptation of these deeply ethical stories. I have tried to keep as far as possible the Eastern point of view, since the book is sponsored by one of the foremost of Oriental Scholars, Dr. Rhys Davids, who has helped me with his advice, and taught me the spirit of the whole conception.

THE HARE THAT RAN AWAY

THIS is the only story I have completely re-adapted for quite small children. and I have found it among the

most popular. I often tell it in connection with Hans
C. Andersen's story of the "Scandal in the Poultry
Yard," of which the subject is practically the same:
the first being simple and direct, the second veiled in
gentle satire.

THE MONKEY AND THE CROCODILE

I INCLUDE this story because of the lighter side and
because we cannot hide from our boys and girls that
craft does enter into the question of success as the world
understands it. It is, however, in my mind where the
Buddha is not at his highest level. Perhaps the less
this story is explained the better.

THE SPIRIT THAT LIVED IN A TREE

THIS story I consider to be one of the most beautiful
in the collection. We cannot baldly appeal to the children to think "of the next generation," but this wonderful picture must fire their imagination where the ordinary didactic appeal might fail.

THE HARE THAT WAS NOT AFRAID TO DIE

IN this story it may be necessary to make a few words
of comment on the point of view of the Buddha which
might not be quite intelligible to the child. The fact,
that though he was ready to sacrifice his own body he
had a care for the tiny insects which might perish with
him, has much significance in the story scheme. It
shows not only the letter of the law but the spirit of the

love which prompted him to act, and represents one of the principal tenets of the Buddhist Faith. The whole story is somewhat remote from modern life, but I have found it of great interest to children of different ages, most especially at the time when Fast Days were called for.

THE PARROT THAT FED HIS PARENTS

The dramatic interest of this story appeals to all ages. I have found quite young children enthralled by the adventures of the parrot. I take exception to the lack of poetic justice in the kinsfolk sharing the parrot's reward—but it was necessary to the Buddha's happiness, and if children should raise the question, I should explain it on that ground.

THE MAN WHO WORKED TO GIVE ALMS

The method of alms-giving may not appeal to modern feeling, but the spirit in which the gifts were made rises to wonderful heights, and the deeds are sanctified by the self-sacrifice which brings them about. In telling this story to groups of boys and girls accustomed to the warnings of charity organizations, the different conditions in the East might be mentioned.

We have here the same idea as in the story of the King who gave his eyes. This story seems to lead up to the other, in which the sacrifice is so much greater.

THE KING WHO SAW THE TRUTH

This story may seem at first to be above the plane of the young child. I have eliminated all the physical suffering, because it is not necessary to bring out the real meaning of the story. Older children (whether in years or understanding) will be able to appreciate the beauty of the sacrifice and the exceeding greatness of the reward.

THE BULL THAT DEMANDED FAIR TREATMENT

THE fact that the Buddha insists on a fair wage, not from selfish greed but for the sake of his employer, lifts the story from the realm of the commonplace which the subject might suggest.

THE BULL THAT PROVED HIS GRATITUDE

AN excellent illustration for children of the necessity of kindness to animals, not only from the merciful point of view, but from the practical question of ensuring good work.

THE HORSE THAT HELD OUT TO THE END

THE children will be much impressed by the courage of the horse, and the power of will he shows in accomplishing the task he has set himself. It is the spirit of the soldier at its best and might be cited as displayed during the Great War by individuals from all nations.

THE MONKEY THAT SAVED THE HERD

THIS is one of the most practical stories in the collection, showing that for success in leadership it is necessary to have a quiet mind, a great deal of knowledge, and a firm belief in success. This is the way ogres are outwitted. The frank laying down of his cards, his open declaration of his plans to the enemy, present the Bodisat at his best.

There is an unconscious note of humor in this tale, in presenting a monkey as possessed of such complete self-control as to be able to bring about so great a miracle, but if any explanation is offered in the telling of these tales, it should be that, whatever the outward form, the Buddha preserves the attribute of a god.

THE MALLARD THAT ASKED FOR TOO MUCH

ORIGIN of the "Goose that laid the Golden Eggs"; Pali word for golden goose is Hansa, whence Gans, goose.

THE MERCHANT WHO OVERCAME ALL OBSTACLES

FOR encouraging a spirit of enterprise, and courage under difficulties, this is an admirable story. I think both boys and girls will apply it (unconsciously) in their everyday undertakings, but this will depend largely on the manner in which it is told: it must appeal to the imagination through the dramatic presentation.

THE ELEPHANT THAT WAS HONORED IN OLD AGE

A SPLENDID example of the honor we ought to show to those old people in the community who have done really good work. This story might be taken in connection with stories from history illustrating the same point.

THE FAITHFUL FRIEND

A STORY which will encourage children's interest in animals and their characteristics, and will increase their interest in observing the ways of those animals under their care.

THE HAWK AND THE OSPREY

THIS story should be told as dramatically as possible, because it is full of action and will hold the children quite breathless. The little touch of the lion objecting at first to be roused at an unreasonable hour is delightfully human, and the fact that when he realizes the necessity he is ready to help, is worthy of his high position among the animals.

GRANDMOTHER'S GOLDEN DISH

THIS story is specially useful because since *rogues* are so often successful in the ordinary sense, and we are bound to admit this ordinary success, it is well that a graphic description of the triumph of honesty should be presented to children which will at once appeal to their sense of fairness.

THE ELEPHANT THAT SPARED LIFE

THIS may seem a little too lofty for the children, but I think it well to include a few stories where the standard may seem too high and the action quixotic. In later years they will realize the philosophy of the story, but the dramatic interest will appeal at once.

HOW THE ANTELOPE WAS CAUGHT

THIS is an admirable treatise on the relative value of things which children are quick to see. It should be told with increasing dramatic force up to the final run of the foolish antelope who has sacrificed his liberty to his greed.

THE BANYAN DEER

THIS is one of the most beautiful of all the Jataka stories. I have given the whole as translated from the Buddhist Birth Stories, only leaving out parts of the description. Any curtailed edition of the action of this story, leaving out the tenderness of the Bodisat for the deer that is "with young," robs the story of its most beautiful meaning.

THE PUPIL WHO TAUGHT HIS TEACHER

THIS is a healthy idea and one which should commend itself to the young who are naturally averse to the idea of Death. It is the opposite of the idea: Whom the gods love, die young.

THE MAN WHO TOLD A LIE

IN this story, if it is considered injudicious to tell children of the hypocrisy of the teacher and the priest,

the title of the man could be left out. For my part, and
from experience as a teacher, I have always found it
wise to admit and condemn the same faults in teachers
and preachers as in the laity, but to point out to the
children that those same faults are the more reprehen-
sible because of the profession which is degraded by
such people as the false priest.

THE CROW THAT THOUGHT IT KNEW

This story shows the power of the skilled workman.
The one who was not skilled thought he could do more
than he had the power to do, and came to grief.

THE JUDAS TREE

The point of this story is the impossibility of a just
judgment without full knowledge of your subject. Each
one has only a partial knowledge and is therefore ex-
cluded from the knowledge of the whole.

THE RIVER FISH AND THE MONEY

The power of honesty restores the lost treasure. The
Bodisatta is not anxious about it, preserves his calm, and
recovers it. Observe the way in which he keeps only the
money which belongs to him, refusing to withhold it from
the dishonest man.

THE DREAMER IN THE WOOD

I have hesitated to include this story as beyond the
range of children but I leave it for the abnormal child
who may value the joy of solitude.

THE RICE MEASURE

THE King falls easily into the trap that is laid for him. His craving for greed leads him to appoint a fool and the fool leads to his failure.

THE POISONOUS TREES

HERE we have the skill of knowledge. The Bodisatta knows how to distinguish the mango tree from the What-fruit tree, and to save the life of those who had eaten therefrom.

THE WELL-TRAINED ELEPHANT

HERE we have the Bodisatta ready to do the miracle that he may convince the King that he is unworthy to possess him. The whole picture is very striking and the story lends itself to dramatic effect.

THE WISE PHYSICIAN

I AM indebted to Sir Robert Morant, K.C.B., who has kindly been interested in the preparation of my book as a whole, for the suggestion that I should include this story (although it is not one of the series of Buddha Re-Birth Stories to which all the others belong), also for the reminder of this special version—namely, the woman's own recognition, through her personal experience, of the impermanence of those things which seem to be lasting.

I should not suggest this story as one which would appeal to children. I have included it for "children of larger growth" as embodying one of the important tenets of the Buddhist Faith, and as showing how personal grief may be assuaged in gaining sympathy with the sorrow of others.

CPSIA information can be obtained at www.ICGtesting.com
Printed in the USA
LVOW07s0959231114

415189LV00002B/282/P